THE POWER OF ADVANCED QUESTIONING

THE POWER OF ADVANCED QUESTIONING

David Tinney, CISSP, Chartered FCIPD

Copyright © 2019 David Tinney, CISSP, Chartered FCIPD

The moral right of the author has been asserted.

Apart from any fair dealing for the purposes of research or private study, or criticism or review, as permitted under the Copyright, Designs and Patents Act 1988, this publication may only be reproduced, stored or transmitted, in any form or by any means, with the prior permission in writing of the publishers, or in the case of reprographic reproduction in accordance with the terms of licences issued by the Copyright Licensing Agency. Enquiries concerning reproduction outside those terms should be sent to the publishers.

Matador
9 Priory Business Park,
Wistow Road, Kibworth Beauchamp,
Leicestershire. LE8 0RX
Tel: 0116 279 2299
Email: books@troubador.co.uk
Web: www.troubador.co.uk/matador
Twitter: @matadorbooks

ISBN 978 1838590 772

British Library Cataloguing in Publication Data.
A catalogue record for this book is available from the British Library.

Printed and bound in the UK by TJ International, Padstow, Cornwall
Typeset in 10pt Helvetica Neue by Troubador Publishing Ltd, Leicester, UK

Matador is an imprint of Troubador Publishing Ltd

This book is dedicated to my wife Tracey and two Children Mali and Aaron who are the most important people in my life. The pleasure in seeing my children grow up and develop have always provided me with the inspiration and motivation to continue to learn and write.

I also dedicate it to all the people who have had to put up with my questions and for answering those questions for so many years.

They all helped me understand the whole skill in questioning presented in the book.

CONTENTS

Foreword ix
Preface xi

SECTION I

1. Advanced Power Questioning — 3
2. What is questioning? — 10
3. Achievement through questioning — 22

SECTION II

4. Advanced Power Questioning – The detail — 67
5. The constituents of questioning — 84

SECTION III

6.	Answering questions	113
7.	Avoiding questions when answering	121
8.	How to become an Advanced Power Questioner	129

SECTION IV

Frameworks for effective questioning   139

9.	Critical Root Questioning	140
10.	Questioning to the Void	153
11.	The Five Whys method of questioning	157
12.	The Kipling Technique	161
13.	Appreciative Inquiry questions	164
14.	The Advanced Power Questioning Framework	168
15.	Advanced Power Questioning Framework in Problem Solving	184
16.	Recruiting effectively using the APQ Framework	187

Summary   194

FOREWORD

My passion for writing continues with my third book. The first, *The Advanced Power State* was a self-mastery book, the second a business book on a new and innovative risk process. This third book goes back to the format so many said was an entertaining read in the first book.

To me a book has to be entertaining in the first instance, informative in the second and provide a thought-provoking opportunity.

The original style was to populate my thinking with little anecdotes and stories of how I came to believe, the knowledge and experience I convey in the book.

As always there are many factors that come into effect to create a book. Those such as the support from my family who I thank for putting up with me and the time taken in writing the book. Also thanks to my son, Aaron, for his diligence going through the book pointing out some changes and to Suzanne Daniels who carried out a full, detailed review of the manuscript before it was sent for final proofreading.

My hope is that, once again, you enjoy reading it and that you gain some real insight into this powerful topic.

PREFACE

What are the real benefits of being an effective questioner?

Over the last twenty-five years I have come to realise the power of questioning and how it helps to provide one of the main foundations for success. As children we pick up the skill quite naturally, if in an environment where others routinely use questioning. However, formal development in question forming or better questioning appears to be rare. In fact until coming to research and write this book I have never had any training or development in these areas.

It was recognising the importance of questioning, the shortfall of skill in this area and the benefits that can be achieved that has motivated me to write about it.

I have taken the subject back to a basic level and decided to build from there. This means you may find it a little easy at the start, however, it is a skill and like any other skill, practice makes perfect, although my son, at the age of eleven, corrected me by telling me that practice makes you better, not necessarily perfect.

This book will explain what questioning is, who does it and why and how it can be beneficial to do it better.

It will also provide tips, techniques and technical approaches, including a new, unique questioning framework that has been proven to work in almost any circumstance.

It will help with making you more effective at questioning. It will help you understand more about how and why others are asking questions. It will also provide you with additional skills for answering those questions more effectively.

In all honesty, it will probably point out some obvious things you already know, but have never really thought about, and will introduce you to some new ideas which can give substantial improvement to your life both at work and leisure.

The book will finish with a section on how "Advanced Power Questioning" fits in with other tools in *The Advanced Power State* (published Feb 2010 – Troubador.co.uk) to make you even more effective at what you do.

A key factor in all of my experience is confidence, and this book will help you build your own confidence through better questioning, and if used effectively will help you to improve your relationships, whether business or personal.

Questioning is invaluable in all walks of life and at all times.

Section I

Section I

CHAPTER 1
ADVANCED POWER QUESTIONING

What are the real benefits of being an effective questioner and following the Advanced Power Questioning Framework?

"The Advanced Power State"

There are two concepts to explore before we get into the exciting tips and techniques where questioning will change your life.

The first is something I call "worldview" and the second is the "Personal Knowledge Base", PKB.

Worldview

I have always believed that each of us, as individuals, creates our own direction through our own individual eyes. I call this our worldview. It is one of the fundamental "keys to success". Knowing you have a worldview, understanding your own worldview and its limitations is vital in your quest for success, but whenever you interact with someone understanding their worldview is also important.

Understanding where another person is coming from, what they think, and how they will respond to you will come from someone's view of the world. Questioning is an effective way of soliciting a person's worldview, of understanding their attitude to something and of delving into their beliefs.

If you understand someone's worldview then you are also more likely to understand their approach to life and many different situations which gives you an advantage at leisure and at work.

Personal knowledge and its immense power
The knowledge we all have is critical to our success but knowledge is not just random information or data alone; it is clearly focused and useable information. I call this refined knowledge store our Personal Knowledge Base or PKB and it is introduced in my book *The Advanced Power State* (Troubador, 2010). It is used in all judgements, influences all actions and is also used to solve problems. It is a precursor to being successful and is something that can be built much faster than people think.

This Personal Knowledge Base gives you huge potential power:

- Social Power
- Emotional Power
- Political Power
- Action Power

The more knowledge you have the more potential power you will have. All you need to convert that potential power is the opportunity and talent to use it effectively. Questioning is one of the most effective ways of converting that potential power into opportunity whilst continuing to build the potential power further, and so read on.

I have used the words "potential power" twice in the preceding paragraph for good reason.

> **Knowledge is not just power**
>
> *I had heard of Francis Bacon declaring "knowledge is power". Initially I used this quote in the courses and seminars I gave for many years until a good friend, Rob, disagreed and argued that knowledge is not power but potential power and that the real power is not just having the knowledge but how you use the knowledge. To use power effectively there are skills in knowing when to convert that potential into real power.*

We will look at how to apply potential power later.

Even now, in a world where information is at our fingertips night and day there is still a requirement for us to have knowledge in our brains. The higher the level of our knowledge, the more effective our capability of doing something becomes. This elevated knowledge also enables us to speak more effectively with confidence and assurance. The more we confer knowledge onto others, the better we will be able to carry out our roles.

It is a fact that the brain loves questions. It loves a mystery! If you ask a question, the brain is trained to seek out the answer using all the available resources you have whether that be your conscious mind or your subconscious mind and the knowledge contained within. Many people can become obsessed with answering questions.

Questioning can also help us to understand. Understanding is, I have always believed, knowing and believing. The receipt of information is only the first stage, the start of the process. But how does this knowledge transition from just information, to being accepted into your knowledge base, and thus becoming real knowledge? Answers to questions allow you to develop a further understanding. They allow you to form your own beliefs about the truth and your worldview, about the truth and your worldview of any subject in discussion.

It is, therefore, with that understanding that we build our Personal Knowledge Base (PKB).

Some important parts of building our PKB include:

- Reading
- Listening
- Reflecting
- Feeling

All of these help with the initial information gathering which is followed by further questioning. These are a key part of starting the process of understanding and believing.

The power of questioning is added to by allowing others to help you achieve greater success by:

- building knowledge through experience, both the use of your own and of other people's experience;
- building better relationships, which is vital to success;
- building confidence;
- building credibility.

Building knowledge through yours and others' experience

Firstly knowledge is not just built from reading, listening, reflecting and feeling. It is so much easier to build knowledge through your own experience. In my success equation first published back in 2010, *The Advanced Power State* (Troubador) shows how pound for pound experience is more impactful than just knowledge when building this Personal Knowledge Base. Drawing on your own experiences is by far the best approach and achieves the best results, faster. Go out and do something; learn it. A complete management industry has been born delivering something called "experiential learning". However, if you cannot experience it yourself, use those around you and draw on their experiences through questioning.

There is an additional benefit from other people's experiences. It is also often a faster way of learning and people are usually very happy to talk about their experiences with someone who is genuinely interested.

Speaking at school

My son went to a school called Woodcote House School. This school, like many others, is very forward-looking and arranges a weekly speaker to come in and talk about a subject. This could be anything from conquering Everest, to the making of Harry Potter. The school often called on parents to talk through their different experiences. I have listed just a few of the speakers and subjects below:

- *How television works*
- *The making of Harry Potter*
- *Alex Abbey-Taylor – Williams Racing*
- *Jamie Berry – TV producer*

> These often captured the imagination of the children but also are examples where the youngsters were able to build their knowledge through other people's experiences.

Talk to the astronaut

On a visit to Kennedy Space Centre, our family went to listen to Wendy Armstrong, a space shuttle astronaut. She was absolutely fascinating and had a remarkable effect on our relatively young children. Her sheer enthusiasm for the shuttle and the Space Programme, despite the fact that this was the day of the programme as we had just witnessed the very last Space Shuttle Atlantis landing, was amazing. The questions put to her by the audience and her answers just left us in absolute awe of such a character. She was a true inspiration to us all on that day.

> ### The Iron Lady
>
> In my younger days, I managed to be in a group audience with Mrs Thatcher in her House of Commons office. WOW, this was a true experience. The sheer passion in the way she answered the questions we put to her was amazing. Whether you agreed with her or not there was a magic around the passion of her belief.

Questioning will help you use your own, but also others' experiences to build your own Personal Knowledge Base.

It is standard knowledge that questioning is a form of communication and will sometimes, therefore, involve more than words. Understanding the words and the dynamic of the communication between individuals will help get the answers needed, whether those answers come through body language or actual words. It, however, goes further than this.

I make a distinction between standard questioning and Advanced Power Questioning. Advanced Power Questioning is based on achieving your purpose by asking questions, in the best way, in the environment in which they are asked. It involves using effective style, the right content and the most effective medium for delivery of questions but it also requires understanding the "Immersed Questioning Environment". Part of the Immersed Questioning Environment, IQE, is the physical environment but it is also the interaction between individuals. It needs the questioner to adapt according to the dynamics between all parties including the questioner, responder and the physical environment, whether that is people, noise, temperature, air or any other input to an individual's senses. It is also the case that the emotions of each individual need to be taken into account as part of this IQE.

This book will take you through a unique technique called the "Advanced Power Questioning Framework" taking you further on your journey to greater personal power.

CHAPTER 2

WHAT IS QUESTIONING?

In the dictionary questioning is defined as "an enquiry". However, for me, it used to come from "the need for an answer", or the "want of some knowledge"; something that is unknown to you at present. Something you do not understand but would like to understand. However, it can be used as a method to help achieve your objectives over and above just improving knowledge.

The first part of this chapter will look at the knowledge side of questioning then the second part will reveal the advanced power of questioning.

Knowledge

It is built into every human psyche to want to know or to be curious, and questioning is one of the most useful ways of satisfying that curiosity.

It does not have to be external questioning, i.e. asking the question of someone else. It may be internal questioning, where you want to know more, and so you ask yourself a question. The information may already be in your head but not put together in the form needed to be extracted or linked for effective use.

Your internal question may well allow you to see external activity relevant to that question and thus be able to help you answer the question.

> **The Matiz**
>
> *A number of years ago my wife needed a new car. We went to the showroom and were looking at the Daewoo Matiz. She only needed a runaround for our new daughter and so a nice small car was ideal. I stated confidently that I had never seen these Daewoo Matiz cars on the road and so they could not be that popular. For the next week, all I saw on the road was this Daewoo Matiz model in all different colours.*

That is the reticular cortex working. Subconsciously your mind will sort out the things that are not relevant to you at the time in favour of those that are. The relevant information will then be brought into your mind's focus and this is easily brought on by questioning.

Questioning can generate improvement.

Any department or organisation that allows and helps its people to become good questioners improves the value within the organisation. A truly fantastic questioner will become better at:

- Leading
- Managing
- Making decisions

- Coaching
- Mentoring

It will improve a person's feeling of importance, self-esteem and belonging helping motivate people and improve engagement. It is also aligned with Maslow's theory of individual needs, where the top of the pyramid is "self-actualisation".

A person skilled at questioning will:

- have more confidence in themselves;
- hold greater self-esteem;
- feel more in control;
- feel a greater sense of belonging;
- have a greater sense of engagement;
- be generally more fulfilled.

Their ability to adapt to new situations will also be improved.

A truly fantastic questioner has a great future ahead of them.

The value of questioning

Questioning provides so much more value than just getting the answers. One revelation is just to realise that most questions are not asked for the answer. This knowledge alone can transform the way you ask and answer questions in the future. It will also help in understanding the power of questions, and the use will be covered more later in the book.

Questioning can curb assumptions

How many teachers ask a question of which they do not know the answer? I assure you not many.

As individuals one thing that we all do is often come to conclusions, making assumptions, sometimes incorrectly, as we go.

Questioning can overturn assumptions and assumptions are something that can regularly get people into difficulties, in both their personal circumstances and their work environment.

> ### The "Land of Conclusions"
>
> *I read a book when I was a child which had a profound effect on me. It was a book,* The Phantom Tollbooth *by Norton Juster, about jumping to the "Island of Conclusions", and it taught me that the land was unreal. Everything in this land was make-believe!*

Whilst it was a children's book the concept has grown with me over the years and I have found that questioning is a very effective approach to challenging those assumptions and getting them double checked before taking a "jump" to a conclusion and into that mythical land.

This book on questioning will enable you to develop your skill and capability driving you to greater success. Some of the techniques will allow you to become a more effective analytical person and once you have the "bug" for this analytical behaviour this need to be analytical will continue to grow the more you use the techniques. I would, at this point, add a word of caution on analytics. An analytical approach is often good and called for as part of any assessment. However, it needs to come as part of a package and that package must also include your "gut" feeling. This comes from your worldview; the experience and knowledge you have gained throughout your life, as well.

Is questioning for good or bad?

Questioning can allow you to show your desire to help others and, as already mentioned, can help build your own self-esteem. It can also have the opposite effect and can crush a person's spirit irrevocably and so I make this note of caution. There is no doubt that questioning can and should be used for the good, however, it can be used for the bad and something I have no desire for any of us to be involved in.

That does not mean it should not be used for exposing behaviour that is not acceptable in our society, something journalists do very well.

An angry MEP

In my youth, I was at a political constituency meeting in Esher, Surrey. At the time there was a group of people who clearly did not consider the member of European Parliament very effective, in fact, some of his behaviour was not appreciated at all. One evening he was speaking to the full constituency and when it was opened to questions this group "one by one" wound up the MEP by asking simple but probing questions which he did not want to answer. It all appeared quite innocent but he became so wound up that he lost his temper and it was only when his wife pulled him down and whispered a few words that he said "I have no further comment on the matter" and sat down. This was all done by very clever but simple distributed questioning.

The book will not only explore how and why questioning can create anger in people, put people's backs up, create defensiveness, but will show how clever questioning can kill conversation depending upon the style, content, and delivery of the questions.

It all depends upon your skill at questioning and your objective in carrying out the questioning, something we will also cover in greater detail later in the book.

It should be noted that depending upon where people sit in their worldview and the approach the questioner takes, the person answering may not want to face the reality that you are opening up to them.

> ### *It's obviously my job*
>
> *I once interviewed, along with two of my colleagues, a top executive for a job. One of these colleagues had invited him to the interview. This "applicant" had worked for our organisation before and was quite sure he would be walking into the position with a friendly chat. I personally did not know him and naturally wanted to know more. I used a technique I call "Critical Root Questioning", something we will look at later, and it was clear that this gentleman was not all he seemed. He became very hostile to me. That hostility did not phase me at all but alienated him from the other two, including his friend. He did not get the position.*

I have found in my experiences over the years that many businesses fail because they do not have the right people asking the right questions politely but robustly enough to get to the right conclusion.

The story of Enron states that the downfall may have been averted if some of the non-executive directors had challenged some of what was going on. I have no doubt! The same appears to apply to the RBS Bank problems in

2009 with many within the organisation not asking too many questions, not rocking the boat, or indeed just turning a blind eye to what was going on.

Indeed the need for structured quality questioning, challenging and debate in a non-personal or hostile manner is vital for success and this challenging can be achieved very effectively by asking questions.

> **The downfall of Margaret Thatcher**
>
> *My involvement in politics was around the time that Margaret Thatcher resigned and it was clear that a major (sorry about the pun as John Major succeeded Margaret Thatcher as prime minister) contributor in her downfall was because she ended up being surrounded by "yes" people. Even on those final days she was being told by her election team, led by a senior MP, that everything was fine and that she did not have to come back from Paris, where she was engaged in the celebrations for the collapse of the Berlin wall, to "twist a few arms" in the tea rooms of the House of Commons. She lost that first internal leadership election but if she had changed just three minds, to vote with her, then the three votes that caused the second ballot would have averted her downfall. There were sixteen abstentions that fateful night and just by changing the minds of three would have given her the 15% majority needed for her to win outright. It would have left us with a very different Britain if that had happened.*

> **The new boy governor**
>
> *I became a governor of Winston Churchill School, St John's, at the age of twenty-three. The head, an old-school type with very strict discipline, observed strong discipline throughout the school even to the governors at governor meetings.*

> *As the "new boy" I was constantly asking questions about the head's recommendations and about other options. It seemed to me that everyone else knew all of the answers but later I realised it was more likely to be just "rubber stamping", accepting without questioning, his recommendations.*
>
> *In one of my first meetings, I asked him to explain one of his recommendations to the governing board and it then became clear that a number of the others in the room also had no real idea about the topic. The following debate meant a lot of work for the head teacher and in this case an overturned decision, well, recommendation really, but it proved to me the power of questions.*
>
> *Some eight years later, with the head retired, a teacher confided in me that the head had thought I had come in to try to take over the school! No, I was just being naturally inquisitive and trying to learn.*

From a very young age then questioning became more and more important to me. In my studies to qualify in human resources, I also began to realise that the basics of people change management can be enhanced greatly by the art of questioning.

Each individual's view, approach, and association can be influenced by questioning and this also allows their judgements to be altered and can sometimes even impact their values.

It showed me that questioning allows theories, hunches, and hypotheses to be challenged and thus can lead to an opening of the mind and to more closely establishing the facts. I have used these techniques personally to prove different hypotheses and deliver full-scale international programmes as well as smaller projects.

As a younger man, I became hooked on the power of questioning as I realised that questioning built on the foundation of my core beliefs and on achieving success, as described in The Advanced Power State.

Is questioning beaten out of us?

Questioning is encouraged when we are very young but, I am sad to say, it often gets beaten out of us by those around us as we get older. I was one of the lucky ones and this did not happen to me. However, it is all too often that the reason the art of questioning becomes frowned upon is the lack of knowledge of the person being asked the question and the defensive retort this sets up.

We have all heard some parents say things like, "that's a stupid question" or "stop asking so many questions" or "all you do is ask questions". The response is usually driven out of insecurity and vulnerability, as they do not know the answers.

> ### Answer the children's questions
>
> *As my children grew up my wife and I always made a great effort to continually answer all of the questions our children posed or to look them up if we did not know the answer. In fact, we would often supplement the answer with as much additional information as possible whilst their interest was alive. We believe that this is an effective way of learning. It sometimes meant admitting we did not know the answer and thankfully, when they were growing up, this wonderful thing called an Internet Search Engine was available. The older days would have seen trips down to the library and endless researching of books.*

Questioning to know more

Questioning has been around as long as we have had enquiring minds. Since the first human or animal was able to reason I believe they were able to question.

It would be great if you not only knew everything there was to know but also that everyone else knew everything they wished or needed to know.

And wouldn't it be great if you knew that everyone interacting with you had your views and experiences and was going to do everything in the best way for the outcome you needed?

That is not the case in the real world, of course, and whilst it remains that way then there will always be a place for questions.

Questions give you the ability to allow a greater level of control and influence over your life and others.

There is one other point, often missed in discussing questioning, and that is handling questions that are put to you in an effective way. This is a skill that you really cannot do without, especially as you rise within an organisation.

Through my many years of teaching public speaking, working in companies on the FTSE and smaller companies as well as my experience through my political involvement in the UK, I have learned that we have to answer questions on our feet and answer them in a way that is always truthful, but effectively communicates our message as well.

As an example:

> **No, we don't charge**
>
> In the UK, at the time of writing, it is a fact that state schools are not allowed to charge school fees. There are, however, a few state schools that have mandatory "extracurricular activities" which have to be paid for.
>
> If you asked someone if the school charged pupils for going there, two answers are truthful.
>
> "Yes" and then explain that the charges do not relate to the educational delivery but to mandatory extracurricular activities. This is absolutely the truth but the sound bite and perception would remain as "yes". The other answer is "No, there is no state school that charges school fees in the UK including Xxxx School".

Both are truthful.

Each answer will allow the questioner to take away a slightly different message and hence questions are always asked within a context, an environment, as mentioned earlier.

The next chapter will work through what can be achieved and how it can be achieved through questioning but I want to leave this introductory chapter with one thought.

Look at the power that a counsellor has and the enormous benefit counselling can bring to people. This is mostly done through questioning.

Simply put questions are a springboard to knowing more, understanding more and thus being able to achieve more.

As with all skills, there is the choice of using questioning more effectively or ignoring it. If you are ignoring it the person next door may not be and could therefore rapidly overtake you.

So, if you think your ability to learn, to do better, and to be more successful is still active then read on about questioning. If not, put the book down now.

CHAPTER 3

ACHIEVEMENT THROUGH QUESTIONING

Benefits of a questioning culture

All culture, in any organisation, is not just based on the external environment, but is led by the top people in the organisation. I have worked in many countries where the "local" culture is altered by the different nationalities at the top of those organisations. This applies whether it is a head at school or a chief executive officer in a company. A company can improve the performance of the whole organisation by installing a positive questioning culture but it has to permeate from the top down through the whole organisation.

Put down questioning if you dare

I have seen a questioning culture, starting at the top, and it clearly allowed opportunities to be spotted and optimised but I have also attended meetings where someone has asked a question and been summarily closed down, then the same person who closed down the questioner has openly criticised the meeting for a lack of participation and ideas! All in the same meeting!

Embrace questioning

How many courses do you see in techniques for questioning? I did a trawl through my contacts, within human resource groups and the Internet and at the time of writing there were very few except within the counselling, journalism and media area.

As an organisation you should provide training for your people in questioning, give them techniques, approaches and allow them to understand the most effective way of getting to the knowledge or result they require. It is a must to make your organisation stronger.

To start to change the culture people must be praised, rewarded for asking questions and not allowed to be shouted down in meetings. An organisation must also recognise that often having a culture of questioning is a paradigm shift, and thus everyone will require significant changes in the way they think. It may be uncomfortable for some managers but the paradigm shift is worth doing.

Indeed it is essential that your organisation finds high-level answers to critical questions and communicates those answers to be successful. Questions such as:

- What is our primary objective or purpose?
- What do we want our values to be?
- What are our unique selling points?
- What are our strengths?

- What challenges us?
- What motivates us?
- What inspires us to achieve?
- How engaged are our people?
- How creative are we?
- What is our track record?
- How can we make that jump in our next product?
- What is our plan to achieve our purpose?
- What do you intend to achieve, today, this month, this year?

These are all fundamental questions which every organisation, company or even person needs to have answered to increase the success level and have a clear focus on the way forward. It then needs to drive forward and continue to ask those questions as the landscape changes.

A company begins to die the moment it stops asking questions and stops questioning itself.

For many years I have been talking to groups about how each individual person is their own Personal Limited Company, PLC. Now usually they are not a formal company in real terms. However, if you think from a practical element we all have

- Income – the salary or wages you receive whether daily, or monthly and any financial bonus you receive.
- Service or product – this is usually the product or personal services you are offering and includes the work you know how to do and are willing to do.
- Sales – this might be just an interview but often you are selling yourself without even knowing it. A builder might suggest to a friend that he can do something for him. Is that not selling?
- Expenditure – well, we all like to spend money. There are genuine

expenses in living but also in providing the service we provide to our employer such as the travel to work, lunch, etc.
- Finance – we all have to track our finances, keep an eye on our bank accounts, make sure we are only spending what we earn, or if borrowing that we can afford to pay off our borrowings by future earnings. We, as individuals, can also go bankrupt.
- Marketing – do you have a CV (curriculum vitae) or a career overview? If not, why not? This is a marketing tool. Using social media is also a marketing tool. It is getting you known and putting your brand out there.
- Research and development – this is our training and education. It is about improving the service, improving the skills.

The concept of the personal PLC is explored more in my first book *The Advanced Power State*.

Therefore, if you accept that you are similar to a company, as a person, and a company will die when it stops asking questions then it follows that your success begins to die the moment you personally stop asking questions and stop questioning yourself.

The Power of questioning

With questioning comes great power. It will help you achieve results that will lead you to a huge personal performance improvement and more effective leadership.

In my time as a leader in a FTSE 30 company, I found there was always a demand to "get it done", whatever "it" might be. Add the power of questioning to the "get it done" and with that, an enormously powerful individual is created. One who continually adds value to whatever they do.

So why is questioning so powerful and how will it help?

Questioning can:

1) Identify a knowledge gap to be filled
This will be known to you all. The basic principle in asking questions has always been:

- ask a question;
- get an answer;
- fill the gap with information.

This has been the way for years. However, what will be new to you is my V.A.P.E.R framework and the addition of questioning to this model. V.A.P.E.R. is then transformed into a hugely effective tool.

V.A.P.E.R. is a management model I have been teaching for over thirty-five years that works in almost all management work and stands for:

- Vision
- Analysis
- Planning
- Execution
- Review

Section IV, Chapter 14 will cover this and the Advanced Power Questioning Framework in more detail.

2) Be an aid to remembering
Questioning is also a major aid to thinking and to remembering. If you establish a gap in knowledge and ask a question, the gap creates a propensity to remember the information when the gap is filled. This works

because the brain has already generated the associated neural links to remember it.

> **Forming a neural path**
>
> *Some years ago I went to a mind mapping course with Tony Burzan as the speaker. He shared a time-lapsed video of a microscopic neural path being formed. It showed the gap and the associated pathways being made to fill the gap.*

A person will, therefore, remember something much more clearly when it is built upon the inquisitive nature of a question. It again forms a fundamental improvement in your own capabilities to remember things.

If you do not continue to grow your memory capability and cognitive functions they will decline. It is like building muscle at the gym. Research shows that if you do not use your muscles within forty-eight to seventy-two hours they start to regress and disintegrate. Now whilst the number of hours may not be the same for the brain the principle remains constant. The longer you do not use the brain and your memory then the more regression will take place and it is much harder to train to get them back. Keep using them each and every day.

This was a truth I did not appreciate in my youth. It came to me when I returned to study after being away from education for a period of time.

Losing your ability to learn

> **Learning ability can be lost, find it again**
>
> *I was at work for five years before deciding to go back to full-time education and take a qualification in electronics and computer engineering. The first three months were absolute hell. Not only had I a work ethic which said I must complete the job but I had also lost my ability to learn as effectively as all of the eighteen year olds who had come straight from school. Firstly I thought it was just age but slowly I rebuilt my ability to learn and as a by-product decided I would never lose it again, setting a learning course or challenge for myself every year since then! Well, every year until I started writing books.*

When I was writing this book I realised that one of the ways I reinvigorated my brain back to learning was through the simple process of questioning.

Break down complexity

Questioning really helps to break down complexity. Many senior company executives will say they need more people who can take something complex and break it down to more simple digestible elements, whilst still keeping the holistic picture in mind.

I liken questioning to building a jigsaw puzzle; making or finding all the pieces as you go along, discarding the irrelevant ones but then getting to the bigger picture as the pieces are put in place. Filling the gaps sometimes allows the bigger picture to be established without totally finishing the puzzle or finding all of the pieces.

Ambiguity, where things cannot be tied down clearly, is another major increasing factor in our lives and now more than any time we need to be able to deal with and work with ambiguity. Those that can and will find themselves very employable.

Ambiguity and complexity are therefore very transferable skills and the ability to work with them effectively will help in your quest to succeed at whatever you do.

Understand personal vision

Our lives are so busy that we tend to give very little thought to the future. If you ask a teenager what they want to do as a career the number that have thought it through is a lot less than when I was at school and it is well recognised, by very successful people, that having strategic goals written down is one of the most important things an individual can do to join their ranks of success.

When looking at any situation or any picture, things will rarely be clear at stage one. There are always questions which can help it come into focus. The questions allow the bits of the jigsaw to be unearthed or assumptions to be challenged and confirmed. This especially applies when dealing with people.

In my human resources work, I learned rapidly that there are always multiple stories or views of any situation. Even the clearest cases of gross misconduct might not be as clear as they look from the first interview.

> **Each story has different views**
>
> *I was once in a situation where an individual was shouting and cursing at everyone. My initial investigation demonstrated an "out of control" individual. A week later he had to undergo a triple heart bypass operation. The investigation eventually led to the fact he was very unwell! I am happy to say he made a full recovery.*

Never assume

Questioning can rapidly reduce your need for acting on assumptions. There have been so many instances where assumptions have caused problems. It is often that people think they know something. They may not even consider there are any assumptions in what they are suggesting, doing or proposing. I often end up drawing out the famous saying…

How do you spell assume… Ass… U… Me and it does make an ass out of you and me. Go and check it whatever "it" is. Going and checking something is often done by questioning further.

If you start with an incorrect assumption everything that follows will be incorrect.

I wrote a book entitled Transforming Your Business Risk Management Approach (Troubador, 2012), to get people out of the concept of making assumptions. I was told time and time again that things would work out fine because of this or that, which were all assumptions. I therefore developed an approach to challenge assumptions that I came to call Critical Root Questioning, a technique that will be explained in greater detail in Section IV, Chapter 9.

Greater Focus – A clear success factor

One of the overriding capabilities that leads to success is the ability to focus on what is at hand. Over the last twenty years the ability for an individual to focus, on any one thing, has dropped considerably. Asking questions can encourage the process of focusing on something specific without the recipient feeling threatened.

My own ability to focus has remained but only by keeping up the pressure to focus when the mind has started to drift. This has improved considerably with my questioning techniques. It has also helped me to provide clear added value organisations want and need.

I also use questioning to help draw people's attention to things, again in a non-threatening way. Perhaps to complain about something, drawing attention to the complainee, more tactfully, about the problem and allowing them to save face. This usually leads to better results.

Mamma Mia and the railings

A number of years ago I had been invited to a concert. As we took our seats I noticed that the railings were set up dangerously and after finding the manager in charge of support I asked him if he thought this might be dangerous to people as a trip hazard. "Point taken" was his response and they were moved.

He managed to save face and the issue was taken care of.

Becoming the creative leader

Questioning allows an improvement in creativity and innovation which can be very effective when using someone else as a sounding board. The creative element allows you to open up new opportunities and to go in different directions and explore further.

The role of leader and manager is often compared. One of the key differences is a leader tends to have a creative flair and this can help with vision and driving change, as opposed to the manager who keeps things running, often with little or no change.

Empowerment is now essential in leadership and achieving organisational success

Very few people are successful at doing everything on their own. If you are to be successful the people around you need to be empowered by you. What does empowering really mean and can you ever achieve full empowerment? One of the greatest failings in business is the abdication of accountability under the guise of empowerment. My view has always been that empowerment should be given but a healthy overview of progress may be needed and is certainly worthwhile.

Some might say empowerment means just leaving it up to someone to do it after giving them high-level view. In real terms that is probably right but a good leader needs to be helpful in the "Empowerment Contract" as I call it.

The Empowerment Contract is:

- a high-level view of the vision (goal);
- a discussion on the approach;

- agreement on parameters including feedback, advice, help, reporting back and timescale for delivery.

Now some of the contract may not be relevant but nevertheless should be considered.

In my experience the old-fashioned mechanistic leader has been replaced and it is now important to be flexible in leadership and management, however, sometimes people need complete empowerment, sometimes they need guidance and sometimes they still need clear, strong directive leadership but without being dictatorial. Questioning effectively assists in achieving these different styles, as and when they are needed, depending upon the individual and their own personal needs.

There is a great divide in doing something independently and being given specific instruction to do it and how to do it. Giving someone guidance, an objective and totally empowering them can be done without the need for questions from the proposer, however, clarity may need to be sought by questioning for the receiver. Likewise the specific instruction can be given, directing behaviour without questioning. However, one of the most effective ways of guiding people is getting them to come to a conclusion personally. Questioning is a very effective way of doing this and often allows someone's self-esteem to grow at the same time. I cannot count the number of times I have wanted to scold people who just "do not get it"! But instead, I ask a question to guide them to a better answer or at least a more appropriate answer.

So instead of saying "for God's sake do this" I might ask if there are different ways of achieving the objective or if there are other options which might involve or not involve them completing the task. At least the situation can be resolved.

This approach and the Empowerment Contract can generate creativity as discussed before, however, it can also generate fear, pleasure, and pride depending upon the way the Contract is handled.

An open type of questioning can get people thinking beyond their initial thoughts, planting ideas which can grow. Most people remain clearly in their comfort zone and rarely deviate from it unless pushed.

I have a fundamental belief that something positive can always be done in any situation. There are always possibilities. The question I continually pose is not whether it can be done but what is the best way to do it? And how much will it cost? When these two things are known a decision can be made as to whether you really want to do it. Those three answers guide the decision on how to move forward. Adopting the concept of "there are always possibilities" will leave you better placed as other approaches or keeping the status quo often lead to procrastination and non-action.

> ### *Believe in Better*
>
> *For a number of years of my working life, I worked for British Sky Broadcasting, which became Sky PLC. Soon after starting James Murdoch became CEO and I agreed with his philosophy when he said "we eat change for breakfast". In fact throughout most of my fifteen years working as an internal consultant they used and really believed the marketing strap "Believe in Better". This was permeated from the CEO down, strengthening the innovative capability of the company enormously.*

Questioning is powerful in delivering the motto "Believe in Better". It involves continually asking yourself and others: How can we do this better? Faster? More effectively? Cheaper? With added value? And what can we do to give a better product or service to our customer? How do we add further value to our relationships?

Questioning empowers employees and empowerment of individuals is required in the twenty-first century if you are to be successful.

The power of questioning in motivation and demotivation has never been in question.

Effective questioning can enhance motivation and from that personal performance can be improved as well as corporate performance. The most successful way of being able to motivate someone, to overcome barriers, and to get them to follow your lead is to understand their personal drivers. Some people are driven by money, some by fame, health, sex, wealth but until you understand an individual's drivers you are at a disadvantage for both influencing and motivating them and it is by questioning that you can understand more clearly those drivers and how to influence a person.

When two people first meet they tend to ask questions relating to finding things in common. These commonalities then begin to grow as each individual establishes common interests. A relationship tends to get built on these common interests. However, often the culture in the UK is for individuals to hold back from the next step, asking about things that are precious to them or why they do or did something. Why do people hold back? These questions are often left until the relationship grows but it is a much slower approach without asking these key questions and establishing what actually drives someone and thus what really motivates them.

In a work environment what would be the point of offering someone an additional twenty thousand pounds of salary to stay and work in the UK when they want to live with their family in another country? Perhaps providing relocation and private schooling in the UK may be more likely to entice them to stay.

> **Programme manager before your time**
>
> I had a young man working for me as a project manager and he had a burning ambition to be a programme manager in a year! Although talented he was not ready for a programme manager role. One of my colleagues was telling me I needed to increase his money but I knew his only driver was to be called a "programme manager". He left our employ and on the same salary he moved to join another organisation as a programme manager. It was a few years later that we met and he confided in me that he had tried to achieve this position a little too fast as he was not quite ready.
>
> At this time for him and my organisation it was not right to give him the title. He made it in the end though and is well respected as a programme manager.

The human condition loves a mystery and peaking curiosity will often get someone motivated to answer the questions you have. It is the style of questioning, the content of the questioning and the delivery of those questions that will decide whether it is a positive impact or negative impact in motivation. We will discuss style, content and delivery in Section II of the book.

> **Murder Mystery Dining at the Top**
>
> In 1995, I wrote a murder mystery play for a small theatre in East Horsley, Surrey called The Nomad Theatre. This murder mystery Dining at the Top played to a full house and generated hundreds of questions coming from all directions trying to get to the same result. Who was the murderer and why?
>
> The questions raised taught me further about the diversity of approaches to questioning whilst following some basic rules.

ACHIEVEMENT THROUGH QUESTIONING

> *The sheer motivation and enthusiasm of those taking part was heart-warming to me, the writer, and of course to the very talented cast and crew who turned a mediocre script into a fantastic performance.*
>
> *The cast had really got into their characters well and so were able to give very credible answers which maintained the storyline and enabled the whole event to remain intact and not crumble around me.*
>
> *Everyone agreed it was a fantastic event.*

A key element of motivation is overcoming any barriers that people have to avoid going in the direction you want them to go in. Understanding those barriers is the first part of overcoming them and it is using questioning that allows those barriers to be understood.

"To understand people's motivation there is a need to understand their drivers."

> ### *For heaven's sake, why do you not follow the process?*
>
> *I was having a discussion with a colleague called Paul who was complaining that a group, within the company, kept ignoring the process and doing it their own way. My first advice was that there is always a reason why people do things. Find out those reasons, those drivers, and then there is a chance to change the behaviour. Paul came back to me later in the day, said he had found out their drivers and told me that they had immovable deadlines and always found there was no time. That's when Paul could get in and help them with additional resources helping them as well as solving his own lack of compliance problem.*

When trying to understand someone's drivers and worldview I ask questions and use a process I call the "Process of the Five". Take the five most likely possible drivers, hypotheses or theories and investigate them, eliminating where it is possible to eliminate. Then take the most likely and consider them further with questioning. If it becomes likely it is not a driver then put it to one side. There is no reason why, subtly, a question cannot be placed by asking directly whether or not that is a key driver. You will very quickly be able to come to a reasonable conclusion as to their drivers.

The same applies to understanding how someone will respond to a question. Analyse it yourself before asking. How could you or would you feel if asked the question? Give yourself five possible responses and optimise the question to minimise any negative possible reaction. This will make it more likely you will get the response you require.

The same applies to influencing as motivation. You want to get something done, feel free to bark orders. That approach would have worked in the 1970s and 80s but groups like the Millennials, those reaching young adulthood in 2000, post-Millennials and subsequent generations have completely changed that approach and now want and need to be more involved in decision making. How do you get them to make the right decisions; to influence them and lead them to the right decision whilst maintaining your own ability to move your position if the influencing has the reverse effect and the answer of the questioning changes your own view? You should always be open to changing your own position by others' responses.

Influencing, like motivation, is improved by understanding barriers and breaking them. Remember people have their own worldview which drives their actions, behaviours, thinking, position, and view, on any subject.

The political debate

In my early political involvement, I found myself working with others to teach future politicians and one of the key elements was to be able to debate. I thus learned to deliberately engage people in debate and so think about everything from an opposing angle. Little did I know how this would build my later questioning capability by opening our horizons to different possibilities and worldview.

Morale also impacts motivation. If morale is low motivation will usually be low. Questioning can drastically impact morale as well as motivation. A consideration in questioning is what someone might read into the questions that are to be posed.

In my opinion, it would be quite improper for a manager to go into a staff meeting and inquire as to why there are so many people without enough work and whether everyone is needed. Trust me, this kind of behaviour goes on. It would be better to question more subtly and understand the situation without making any rash judgements or decisions. If the circumstances needed a review of this kind it is important to keep positive morale and put people's minds at rest.

In many organisations restructuring is done badly and morale takes years to rebuild. In many instances this does untold damage to an organisation actively disengaging people. It really does not have to be that way if it is carried out in a fair and sensitive manner. Both achieve the restructuring but one approach keeps those left in the organisation much more engaged with the company and its purpose.

Encouragement is needed by all – encourage people to decide or act

Empowerment, engagement, and influence are all fine but one of the weak points in many organisations is paralysis, due to a lack of decisions. In all walks of life and different organisations I have seen great examples of effective decision making but those who are paralysed and not able to make decisions will always reach a certain level and go no further. This may be linked to the "Peter's Principle" where people rise to their level of incompetence. I have been challenged on whether making a good decision is more important than taking a decision. I personally have found that those who do make decisions, whether good or bad, are always more successful. Most good leaders and managers recognise that occasionally decisions may not always be perfect and are willing to change and adapt later if needed.

Fulfilling Commitments

I was working with volunteers, at a theatre mentioned earlier called The Nomads, for many years. At the time I looked into why people did not do things they had committed to do. I found some interesting results which are relevant here. The most common reasons were:

- *•not knowing/remembering it needs to be done;*
- *•not knowing how to do it;*
- *•not knowing how to start it;*
- *•not having it as a priority so they would say "no time".*

Which do you think was the most common?

Not knowing how to start it

I refer to it as the "Blank Sheet Syndrome" or BSS for short. Confronted with a completely blank sheet many people will not be able to get something started and will procrastinate indefinitely. If a leader carries out a follow-up shortly after agreeing with someone for something to be done, perhaps with some words of advice to "kick start" the initiative they are more likely to overcome the inertia. In my experience they will find it really does achieve better results and quicker as well as generating greater loyalty with the individuals concerned. Ninety-nine times out of one hundred this gives a great result and is far better than the scolding for not achieving it.

Ask yourself, "Why would someone not do something they agreed to do?". Most people would come to the more negative conclusions such as, well, they cannot be bothered. The number of times I have heard this said is just too many to document. It rarely is because they cannot be bothered. Understand the barrier.

Motivation Framework

- Not knowing/remembering it needs to be done – remind them.
- Not knowing how to do it – get someone who knows how to support them.
- Not knowing how to start it – provide guidance.
- Not having it as a priority so they would say "no time" – guide priorities or relinquish the task to someone else explaining why.

Energising people is not just about encouragement

Energising people can be classed as part of motivation but I look at it slightly differently. People can be motivated but lacking in energy. In my success equation, Advanced Power State, I have an "e-squared" which represents energy and enthusiasm, because the difference in results from someone with an abundance of energy on what they do and achieve can be incredible.

There is also another benefit of energy and enthusiasm. It rubs off on everyone around them and generates a real magnification of performance from others as well. Look at a group, any group and the person with that "e-squared" will be the person others flock to.

Research says confidence is lacking in the Millennials and Post-Millennials but what about everyone else?

Questioning is a key technique in allowing your confidence to grow but also allowing another person's confidence to grow. This is the solid foundation for good coaching. Coaching is not about telling people but about bringing out of them the answers that already lie within.

If the questioning is done well in the style, delivery and content of the question being asked, then the confidence and credibility in the questioner are increased but clearly, if the questioning is poor then confidence and credibility can be reduced.

> *Performing at your performance appraisals*
>
> As a human resources specialist, I have often had to carry out appraisals. The way you communicate a "could do better" message is important. I was in a meeting some time ago with a gentleman who was not really performing in a number of areas. With gentle questioning such as "How did others react to you when you told them it needed to be done overnight?" or "Are there any ways that it could have been communicated more effectively?", it allowed him to come to his own conclusion that he needed to work on his communication.

So telling someone they are wrong will never be as useful as getting them to reach that conclusion themselves. Questioning can help you achieve it. However, I should not mislead you. There are times, at performance appraisals, when you just have to say it and say it straight even if it is not pleasant to hear.

Having better relationships with people leads to more performant collaboration

We know relationships with people involve commonality as visited earlier in this book.

The power of people working together is also well known and yet, often because individuals have their own agenda, collaboration is not always good.

Questioning can improve collaboration and build on relationships. As covered earlier it is often questions that not only allow the first steps in building a relationship but the continuing of a growing relationship. The introduction is often by a question and helps the developing of the commonalities between two people that allows the relationship to thrive. It is by sharing what you are, what you know and your experiences that another person manages to establish those common interests and thus helps relationships grow.

However, only genuine interest will allow the experiences to be shared in full and the knowledge gained.

So next time you are talking to someone, stop talking and listen, and listen, and listen.

Build your knowledge through their experiences and further align yourself with the Advanced Power State.

How do you know which way to go without clear direction?

A critical part of leadership is giving clear direction. Making decisions is, of course, a part of it as is empowerment. However, clear direction needs to be received, not just given.

As a leader you need to know that the direction has been received by the audience it was given to.

Questions help clarify the direction given and that it has been received. This can work both ways too.

"Would it be kinder to everyone to…"(then give the direction). For example, "Would it be kinder to everyone to announce it at the next meeting?".

"Is the (… direction…) the right course of action?" Is announcing at the next meeting the right course of action?

It is also possible to continually use summary questions. They can be very powerful in understanding whether the correct communication has been received. Examples like:

- So what are your thoughts on that plan of action?
- Is that the right way to go?
- Is there anything further?

These are all quick questions but you can use longer questions, if needed. Some would refer to these as open and closed questions and I will explain more about this later. Other examples could be:

- Can you take me through what that means for you then?

- Are you able to give me a little detail on how you might take that forward at a local level?
- Where would you start on something like that?

Overcome obstacles that block your way

Throughout life, there are people who will always block what you are trying to achieve. Live with it.

Most people suggest it is sensible to get annoyed and complain, and rightly so. Well, rightly so in some circumstances. Before complaining always decide the value to you or others of making those complaints and make sure it is worth the work. Complaining, however, is also unlikely to cement a longer-term relationship, but there might be no need for a longer-term relationship.

There will always be people who just will not move. Even when their drivers have been found they may still stay fixed to save face.

I have found only four ways of attending to obstacles:

- go around them;
- go through them;
- go over them;
- go under them.

On the surface none of these requires questioning but each of these leads to confrontation unless done with the person at your side and supporting the direction. Please do not misunderstand. I believe that confrontation has a very important place and role in business but it does not have to be the whole story and it should always be professional confrontation and not personal confrontation.

Work it through with the individual by de-personalising the obstacle. Get the individual to understand there is an obstacle in the way of everyone achieving their objectives and that can be done via leading questions.

- Is this an obstacle to us moving forward?
- How could we move around this obstacle?
- Can you or anyone else help with this obstacle?
- Is this an obstacle to us moving forward or just a perceived obstacle?

As a leader you need credibility – this will help achieve it.

Leaders who ask questions tend to make better decisions because their information is more complete.

It is acknowledged, by most, and covered earlier that good decisions lead to success. It makes sense that people are more likely to follow leaders who make good decisions.

Good decisions come from having the courage, knowledge, and experience to be able to make those good decisions based upon a top-up of any further knowledge that is needed from asking questions.

The quality of the questions you ask can also show your followers the in-depth knowledge you already have in the subject area. My experience has shown that someone asking a good question demonstrates talent and knowledge, which, in itself, builds credibility. Even admitting you don't know the answer usually brings better information to make a decision and can build trust and credibility.

> **Questions from the young**
>
> I spoke at one of the lecture nights at a boys' prep school called Woodcote House on the subject of broadcasting.
>
> After my presentation, these very young children aged from seven to twelve, bombarded me with excellent questions; questions that in my view were well beyond their years. How long is the biggest satellite? How much of that is solar cells? How does a 3D system work in a cinema? And the questions kept on coming. They showed credibility of themselves but also the school.

Influencing people through questioning remains key

Questioning is an effective tool for altering attitudes, opinions, thoughts and beliefs. The discussion from questioning, bringing out further information, further knowledge, bringing people's ideas together and sparking new ideas, is the foundation for changing people's attitudes and even their beliefs. It can cause someone to change their worldview as, remember, each of our worldviews is built on the foundation of knowledge and experience.

The new toe-protected shoe style!

I think worldview became obvious to me when I was a director of a manufacturing company and I was running the HR and production facilities. I was in charge of the health and safety and I instigated a new rule in the factory that everyone had to wear toe-protected shoes. Most complied very quickly and I provided them with a free, company-paid, pair of toe-protected shoes. However, eventually I was down to one lady. On a cold winter's morning, I remember it so well, she "crashed" into my office and declared she could not find any shoes to her style. I reached for all of the three main-supplier catalogues and she paged through every single page. At the end, she declared, "I still cannot see any I like. None of them are sandals!" My jaw hit the floor and after thirty minutes of explaining the whole point of the protective shoes was to enclose and protect the toes, I still could not change her worldview. She was given duties that did not need toe-protected shoes, but for me, it confirmed my view from politics that there are different worldviews and concepts in all walks of life with all people.

I just want to get smashed!

I carried out an appraisal on a factory worker. As part of this appraisal, I asked where he wanted to get to in the next three to five years. What were his ambitions? He stated: "Look, mate, you just don't get it. I come in at eight on Monday. On Friday I get paid, go to the pub and get smashed. On Saturday I go down the pub, watch the footy, get drunk and have a few cigarettes (I changed the word). On Sunday I watch the footy and spend the rest of my money getting smashed and then go back to work Monday, skint and ready to start the week over. I like that and that's all I want to do."

As a younger man, I thought this was a short-sighted worldview and I struggled to comprehend it. Why did he not want to better his life? It reinforced further my belief in the worldview concept.

It is by understanding each person's worldview that you know where to start influencing people through questions and directing experience and knowledge their way.

Influencing is something we do every day and is part of the human condition. Persuading, calling attention to better, altering attitudes and worldviews all sit in the same arena.

Questions bring ideas and thoughts to the top of the brain. The thought process itself is often enough to get the mind working on the problem or thinking through the current challenge.

Once someone is thinking of the targeted subject the questioning can be made more leading and thus can start to influence the individuals further. Continuing to challenge the closed view and putting through other options which logically and emotionally link back to an individual's drivers and needs will be key.

What is the first thing that is taught on a sales course?

Understand the customer's needs. Success in sales comes from matching the needs of the customer to your product or service.

Some salespeople would draw a difference between the perceived need and the real need.

One has to remember the emotional part of selling and indeed decisions overall. Experts will say that buying a car is 80% emotion and 20% logic. They will also say that men specifically will seek to justify the 80% emotion with logic post-decision.

To influence, then, start people thinking about different things, different angles, with different approaches by asking great questions.

Provide a completely different picture, maybe even an abstract picture

Assist people in changing focus, altering attitudes and worldview; persuading and motivating all through questioning.

> ### Giving advice to teenagers
>
> *My son and daughter both went through phases, as we all do, of not wanting to take advice. The only way I was able to give advice was to ask questions and for them to come to their own conclusions.*
>
> - *Are you likely to work harder if you are happy?*
> - *Which college are you likely to be happier at?*
> - *What are the advantages over other colleges?*
> - *Are there any disadvantages of this college?*

I am sure you will not have overlooked the subtly here. What are the advantages over other colleges? This leads the questioner to subconsciously realise there are advantages and to look for them. If you ask are there any disadvantages of this college, it will lead them further to think of the disadvantages.

Even the order in which the questions are asked is leading.

Are you likely to work harder if you are happy? Yes… This is the first positive response. Which college are you likely to be happier at? XXXXXX College. Now the individual has related happiness with the college they have just mentioned. On a subconscious level, a leap has already been made.

Woking campus

In 2007/2008 Woking Council put out a survey called "Campus Woking". This was an incredibly good piece of propaganda. The idea was to lead people to agree that three different schools should join together to become one and that children would walk or be bussed from one school, when doing maths, to another which had science labs to another with sports facilities. This meant a reduction in the expensive facilities at each individual school. The challenge was in the questioning.

The survey went through each question meaning any sensible person would have to answer "Yes" even though you disagreed fully with the overall concept.

These were not the exact questions but similar:

Would your child like a laptop for £1? How can you say no to that?

Does your child want a good education?… Errr, who is going to say no to that?

Do you want good quality science facilities and a specialist centre for your child to achieve in the sciences?

And the questions went on.

> I was so enraged with the approach that I personally took it up with the council, not because I believed one thing or the other but that it was so biased that it would never represent what people actually thought. In the end I was told the council did not use it and certainly the schools did not join together.

Conflict needs to be the root of good, not bad – resolve conflict better.

In all the years I have been working as a leader and manager both before and after studying HR I have been amazed so many people avoid conflict. Why?

Conflict is a part of the human condition. I do not believe in avoiding conflict unless, as mentioned earlier, the conflict is personal. Business conflict is needed and I do not take professional conflict personally. I do accept, though, that in many of my experiences it is clear that the conflict is not meant to be personal but is still taken to be by the receiver.

Personal conflict, in a work environment, is bullying and not acceptable but if we agree that should not happen we should not shy away from the fact that several individuals in a room are not always going to agree with each other. In fact, for a healthy organisation there needs to be disagreement, different approaches and different worldviews. Working out how to drive through conflict to add value is the secret to making it a success and again questioning comes forth. It is here that mediation also comes in.

Enabling effective mediation

Mediation is really only needed when the conflict gets out of hand.

The power of mediation benefits enormously from the skilled questioner.

Understanding the different points of view can really only be gained from the effective questioning of the parties involved and then the distilling of the important points prior to finding common ground upon which agreements can be built. Often by the time mediation is called for the different parties are at each other's throats and so it is the gentle, careful, non-threatening questioning by "an independent party", a trusted party, that will allow the common ground to be built. Those that are effective mediators can achieve this.

To get the most from meditative questioning there has to be trust and objectivity.

If by questioning trust and transparency are not demonstrated then mediation will fail. Choose your words carefully.

A mediator is a key partner in business

So how do you resolve conflict between different parties?

I am often brought into situations to mediate. Why me? Because I can stay detached, asking objective questions even when people are at each other's throats. My experience in questioning along with the frameworks and approaches all work well together in mediation. These frameworks are covered in detail in Section IV.

Recognise your worldview as one of the most important assets you have – use it better

We are nothing if we do not understand our own worldview. It can be said others will think we are nothing if we don't communicate our worldview but both are applicable.

I agree if you do not have a view do not present it. Whether that be at a meeting or in a personal situation. But ask yourself why do you not have a view? Is it a lack of information?

If it is then get the information you need. If, on the other hand, it is lack of information and you have no interest in the subject then question your role in being there. I am not really a football supporter and sometimes, therefore, I do not know enough to have a view. My response is exactly that. I remove myself or excuse myself.

Provide me with some knowledge and I will very quickly have a view and that will be based upon my own knowledge and experiences from my past.

Questioning subtly allows you to either find out more information, to have a view or like influencing, further push forward what you think and this itself can help to influence others.

Invoke that emotional response from others

Questions often invoke an emotional response as much as a logical response. To know why is to understand human behaviour, the Immersed Questioning Environment, and the worldview of the individual. As part of your planning, you need to decide whether you actually want an emotional response and how you will move forward if you get an unwanted emotional response.

Is the person/audience likely to have an emotional response? This becomes part of the consideration at the planning stage. I can hear screams of "I don't plan every question I ask". My answer to you is why not? It takes seconds to give some thought as to how people might take the questions you are asking and eventually, as the questioner, your planning becomes automatic.

So how can I prevent the response from being emotional? The short answer is to change the content, style or delivery. This will be covered in later chapters.

How can I mitigate the unwanted response should it come to pass? The first part of this battle is to understand there is an unwanted response.

An example is telephone conferencing. I find it much more difficult to read someone. Video conferencing, if poor quality, is not much better. Telepresence or other more high-quality telephone conferencing can make the difference. Either way, the emotional response is shown through body language and especially the eyes which continue to be a window into the soul.

Once you understand there has been a response, half the battle is complete. Next, think on your feet and narrow down why the emotional response is there and allay the root of that response.

Look for these emotion responses when questioning and adapt to them:

- Sadness/Sorrow
- Happiness/Pleasure/ Enjoyment
- Pain
- Pride
- Fear/Fright
- Envy
- Anger
- Love
- Hope
- Respect
- Wonderment
- Amusement
- Courage
- Pity

- Patience
- Appreciation
- Despair

Remember the eyes! Body language will always help but the one place you will always see emotion is in the other person's eyes. Look into other people's eyes, in a non-staring, non-threatening way, when you are talking to them. The feedback is very useful.

Take action on that emotional response in line with your overall purpose or objective.

Achieving more through coaching

Questioning is a major part of coaching. What is coaching? Many would say the definition of coaching is "The process of training someone to play a sport, to do a job better or to improve a skill".

The official dictionary definition of coaching is:

"A process for learning and development to occur to improve performance" or "a one to one relationship where an individual uses skills as a vehicle to work through issues in a structured way to find an outcome or solution".

For me, however, coaching is about bringing a skill or ability out of individuals. Creating the understanding from within as much as externally.

A number of books discuss different techniques in coaching and it is out of the scope of this book to cover in great detail. However, questioning is so powerful in coaching that there is a place for it here.

Directive Coaching

Coaching has an objective to improve someone's capability, to guide them on moving forward and to generally improve their skills. This should be done in a planned way and I often disagree with purist coaches in that I carry out what I call "Directive Coaching". This is coaching which, as its title alludes to, has some degree of direction being fed into the coaching session.

The first part of this Directive Coaching is to ensure that the environment is conducive to coaching. A cold, noisy environment is not ideal. A warmer environment with comfortable chairs is more likely to bring out the positivity that is needed.

- Step 1 is thus: "Create the right environment".
- Step 2 "Decide the required outcome from the coaching".

Think, write down what you are trying to achieve; what is the outcome or objective of the coaching session?

The outcome may be yours or the coachee's. This needs to be resolved unless you both have the same outcome or both can be achieved. So what do they want to achieve from the session and is it aligned with your own objectives? Can you achieve both outcomes?

Whether the coaching is voluntary or "required" might also affect the outcomes. The coaching has to be done positively with both individuals taking part after all.

There is a need to agree with the coachee on what the goal is and the outcome expected, at the starting point of the session. Until you both agree these the coaching cannot continue.

Step 3 "The starting topic". Once you are clear on the outcome or outcomes then the starting point needs to be decided. What will be the topic for the opening questions? Once underway this is likely to move considerably but the opening is key to reaching the end outcome and needs to be carefully planned.

Once you have considered the environment, outlined an outcome and decided the starting point, the next stage is to plan the questions you are to use and the style, content, and delivery. I will discuss more about these and open and closed questions in Section II Chapter 5 later in the book, but coaching requires open questions, questions which solicit a longer response than just yes or no.

- Step 1 – "Create the Environment"
- Step 2 – "Decide the required outcome"
- Step 3 – "Decide the starting topic"
- Step 4 – "Plan the questions"
- Step 5 – "Execute the coaching session"

It is now the skill of the coach that will take the person through the questions, answers and follow-ups to help bring out of them the required skill.

It is the additional use of leading questions where the Directive Coaching is demonstrated. It is the skill of the individual coach that will decide just how much direction is needed and less is often more. However, it is about getting to the goal or outcome in the most efficient and effective manner and helping those see the new skill that makes it all worthwhile.

With coaching, there is no shame in stopping and taking a break, regrouping and revising your plan if things go a little awry. My timings are based on a fifteen-minute break every forty-five minutes with a clear summary of where the session has reached just before the break.

Remember though, even with Directive Coaching, you are not solving a problem yourself, you are guiding and leading someone, taking them on their own internal journey. So they need to do the majority of the talking. However, part of the Directive Coaching is to challenge constructively as the coaching is underway.

A coach should be completely familiar with the type of open questions that give the best results. In any coaching session, I would use questions such as:

- Tell me about xxx.
- Tell me more about xxx.
- What do you think?
- Are there any or what are the options?
- How could you deal with it?
- What do you think is stopping you?
- Why do think it is stopping you?
- Was that something you have done before/seen before?
- What would be the likely outcome of…?
- If there are no barriers what could you do?
- How could you overcome the obstacles or barriers?
- If there were no barriers what could be your next steps?
- How could you do it differently next time…?
- If you were advising someone else what would be the first step?
- Can you explain more about it?
- What do you think needs to be done?
- How does that work?
- Can you break it down to more simple steps for me?

It is important with any coaching to listen, listen and then listen some more.

I introduce the concept of "Active listening" in *The Advanced Power State* (Troubador, 2010). Coaching benefits from the Active listening tools which include paraphrasing and summarising back to the individual at regular stages in the session.

It is not changing what has been brought out but playing back, summarising accurately to the individual. This shows your understanding but also plays back to the individual what has been said for them to think further and to reinforce the thoughts have come from them.

Clarifying questions are also an excellent approach to playing back ideas that have been presented. "So do you mean…?"

A question such as "Is that an accurate summary?" allows them to come back and correct you if you have misunderstood anything but also allows you to understand whether or not you are making progress towards your objective.

Remember to use non-verbal communication as well as the answers in your analysis, and for the summing up.

When your coaching session begins to get towards the outcome then the session needs to be closed down, again with open questions as to the actions that are to come out of the session.

The whole point of the coaching is to take the individual or team from one place to another and the actions that follow will be the "real" result from the coaching session.

In summary then the steps for Directive Coaching are:

- Step 1 – Create the environment
- Step 2 – Decide the required outcome
- Step 3 – Decide the starting topic
- Step 4 – Plan the questions
- Step 5 – Execute the coaching session
- Step 6 – Open the coaching session with start topic
- Step 7 – Summarise with a leading element if needed

- Step 8 – Analyse the feedback, verbal and non-verbal
- Step 9 – Assess the move towards the required outcome
- Step 10 – Close off the coaching with a clear agreement on achievement and actions
- Step 11 – Summarise actions and next steps

In coaching it is imperative to keep the dialogue going and Directive Coaching makes this easier as it provides the means to add in ideas. Coaching is about clarifying in the person's mind and them finding their own direction.

As much as I recommend Directive Coaching there are other models too. One I recommend is "Effective Coaching" – Myles Downey Cengage 2003. Here he describes a great framework for more conventional coaching.

- Topic
- Outcome
- Reality
- Options
- Wrap Up

Questioning in coaching can close people down if used incorrectly. It can lead people rather than let them come to their own conclusion and if too personal can impair the emotional well-being of an individual. Take care.

The problem of problem solving – personally and in business

Approaches to problem solving are explained in Section III but to me, problem solving is one of the holy grails of success and yet the foundation for effective problem solving comes from the effectiveness of asking questions.

From the clear vision of how the landscape will be once the problem is solved, the "goal" if you like, to the clear articulation of the actual problem, questioning is involved.

Problem solving usually fails on either the lack of real understanding of the problem or inadequate facts to be able to come up with clear solutions.

Answering questions, of course, is one of the key ways of being able to get both facts and understanding.

I often equate problem solving to building a picture, getting an answer via;

- gathering facts;
- making judgements;
- testing hypotheses;
- narrowing possibilities;
- closing down red herrings;
- exploring leads.

And different questioning is needed at each stage.

In Section IV I will present problem solving using the Advanced Power Questioning Framework. This framework is a powerful tool in you becoming successful at whatever you wish to do, including solving problems.

Summary

Achieve through questioning
This chapter was designed to take you through the real power of questioning and just how it can help lead you to success. If you have come away having

confirmed or created a view that questioning can improve your capabilities at leisure and work then it has achieved its aim.

Section I has given you an insight into the power of questions, where they can be used, how you can benefit from asking questions and just how much more powerful you can be if you learn to really enhance your capability in this area.

It has also introduced how it links in with the Advanced Power State.

Section II will cover more detailed questions and questioning itself. It will explore the Immersed Questioning Environment, it will help you understand more the relationships and how they affect questioning and will cover detail of the types of style, content and delivery of questions.

Section II

Index

CHAPTER 4

ADVANCED POWER QUESTIONING – THE DETAIL

Before moving to Advanced Power Questioning, APQ, here is a brief summary of some of the key points from Section I to better understand Section II.

To understand Advanced Power Questioning you need to understand worldview, a concept we looked at earlier in the book and went into in more detail in *The Advanced Power State* (Troubador, Feb 2010).

As much as our own life is centred around our own worldview and we see everything through this worldview the responder will centre their life around their worldview.

Each individual will have a different worldview based upon the knowledge and experience gained since they were born. Other people's worldviews will need to be further understood for someone to be successful at forming the right questions obtaining the answers that are needed.

As well as worldview a good questioner needs to appreciate that the person responding to a question is also living within an external environment and this will influence the responses given. I cannot stress how much understanding the environment is critical to a questioner's success.

If you were to ask a person "How is your father?", a perfectly normal, innocent question, most people would answer with little emotion, however, if he was very ill or had died recently it is likely to initiate a very emotional response. This response, a little extreme in my example, is independent of the words and will give you some clues to the fact something in the environment around is different to that which you probably expected; if, of course, you are tuned into the response.

This is all part of the Immersed Questioning Environment in which Advanced Power Questioning lives.

The Immersed Questioning Environment

Questions are always asked within the Immersed Questioning Environment. This does not only mean the location and ambience of where the question is asked but also includes detail of the person and how they are disposed at the time of the question.

Factors in the Immersed Questioning Environment are:

- the external physical environment in context to the answer and the questioner;
- the comfort and how the responder is feeling;
- physical and mental state of health of the responder;
- the worldview that the responder has;
- the relationship between the questioner and the responder;

- the type of person who is answering the questions;
- the type of person who is asking the questions;
- the approach to asking the questions;
- the style of the questions;
- the content, including the words of the questions;
- the method of delivery; the way questions are asked and answered.

The External Environment

One way of looking at the external environment is to look at P.E.S.T.L.E.O. This is a common management analysis tool but very relevant here.

- Political
- Economic
- Social
- Technological
- Legal
- Environmental
- Organisational

But anything external can be included.

Political

The external political environment can be world politics, office politics or even individual politics. These external factors can have a major effect on the questioning and answering dynamic. If you ask a question of someone who does not like you or what you stand for, the answer, if you get an answer, will be slanted and may mislead you. This answer can be affected by personal politics but also by political party politics or office politics.

> **The Libyan bombing impact**
>
> I was canvassing voters on the local election trail in the May 1986 local elections at the time of the Libyan bombing by the US forces in April 1986. The attack was carried out in response to the 1986 Berlin discotheque bombing. The US forces launched the attack on Libya from US airbases in England and there was a huge public outcry throughout the UK. I saw the attitudes on the doorstep change from pro-government to anti-government in less than twenty-four hours. In those May elections, the Conservative Government lost 975 local councillors. The answers to who will you vote for changed overnight.

Economic

The economic environment speaks for itself. Someone will view the world differently from a financially stable reference point to someone in an unknown state or near the financial breadline. This is often why politicians get accused of being "out of touch" with the electorate.

The worldview of each individual, regarding the economic impact to the questions and answers, again comes from what they have lived through and experienced. How much they know about the economy, from not only a historical perspective but also a current and personal perspective will also be relevant. In addition the answer will be influenced by their developed knowledge of economics, whether through a specific economic degree or knowledge gained in the "University of Life".

Social

Social pressures in individual relationships always have an effect on the Immersed Questioning Environment as well as changing worldview.

> ### The influence of peer pressure
>
> *I saw a great example of peer pressure with my seven-year-old son. He had been involved in tough activity non-stop through the week with his school, getting only a few hours' sleep on two consecutive nights. On the following day he did not want to attend rugby training, which he loved.*
>
> *I tried everything to get him to go and it was only when I was there and one of his school friends had made it, one of those friends who had done the same work as he had done, did he decide he would go. This peer pressure was enough for him to come down and join in.*

Social peer pressure is a powerful environmental driver

I have often also experienced situations where people would say one thing with certain people around but would clam up or say something different with others around.

Technological

Our technology is also constantly changing. In the 1960s having a TV was unusual.

> ### Landing on the moon
>
> *I remember our family rented a television to see the moon landing on 20th July 1969. It was from Radio Rentals! It was a small picture provided in black and white with a very large casing around the television.*
>
> *In the 1970s mobile phones were all but unheard of and yet today they are seen as essential tools.*

> **Early technology**
>
> I had one of the first Telepoint (Rabbit) services from Hutchinson Telecom in 1992 but analogue mobiles started in the early 1980s and were the size of a brick. Now look at the smartphone or watch in your pocket!

The advancement of technology, from the Sinclair ZX80 to the tablets of nowadays, which even have an interface you talk to, has changed all of our views and the way we live.

In 1970 I flew to Lebanon and it was big deal flying in those days. Now it is almost as common as taking a train and often cheaper.

Technological changes have and will influence our worldview and thus the way we ask and answer questions.

Legal

The legal aspects also change worldview. Legislation often restricts what we can do and drives change. The anti-smoking laws, whether you consider them right or wrong, have helped reduce the number of smokers in the UK. It has also made the UK less tolerant of smokers, even when they are outside. If you venture to the rest of Europe, though, you will find a huge number of smokers, or is it just my perception?!

The anti-smoking laws, however, have contributed to changing the "public house" scene with thousands of pubs closing down in the first decade of the twenty-first century.

Environment

The status of the world and even the weather can change our views and answers to questions. If you want a positive answer to something ask someone, if possible, when the sun is shining and not when there are storms outside!

Global warming or cooling, melting of the ice caps, serious flooding, tsunamis, and earthquakes are all just instances of our environment and will have an impact on the way we answer questions, as well as impacting on our general decision making.

World experience

I have lived through Hurricane George in Florida and through a 4.7 (Richter scale) earthquake in San Francisco. So in the winter of 2013/14 I had already had experience of bad weather when Great Britain saw sustained rain and storms that had not been seen in hundred years including a mini tornado which hit my family in Surrey, England. My worldview already had the knowledge and experience at just how powerful and how much at risk from the incremental weather we all were. I could see building materials tied down but the huge sheets of ply wood were lifted from a stack and started flying around in the air around us. We were already protected from the wood by the protection of a concrete support and alcove we had found.

In the end, our village lost power for thirty-nine hours and I had to turn back from many roads which were just impassable but I had contingencies planned for these sorts of eventualities. Anyone asking me questions on this would have answers based upon those experiences.

Many will have also lived through the storms in the early 1980s across the UK. I was driving back from the south coast of England having delivered a seminar and was literally dodging the tree branches as they were falling around me.

The environment might also be more local than this. If you are in a twenty-four-hour news studio and you are asked a direct question the answer could be different from a one-to-one open discussion.

> **Yes Prime Minister**
>
> *I was interviewed live on Sky News at prime time on the morning of 22nd November 1990 at around 8.20am and was asked the question "Will Margaret Thatcher stay on as prime minister?". My answer was that she would fight on and win, which was publicly what I had to say. At the time there were already internal mumblings that she might resign but I had no choice except to say that she would fight on. Otherwise the interview might well have lost her some support, if she had stayed. If I had been asked on a one-to-one basis the answer would probably not have been quite so firm.*

So each area of PESTLE can play a part in effective questioning but consider how people vary in different environments.

There continues to be different external factors touching someone and at different times of the day, week, month and year and with different emotions. To be successful at questioning you need to try to understand these conditions.

How do you feel when you are not well, have a headache or your mind is on something important other than the questions you are being asked?

I have been a first aider since 1983 and I am amazed that when someone is clearly coughing and unable to breathe properly well-intentioned individuals ask, "Are you all right?".

When a person is not well they may be short-tempered. If someone asked, "Are you all right?" the answer would probably be a civil yes but if someone is having a coughing fit they often will not be quite so polite.

Even whether someone is interested in what you are asking will affect how they feel.

> ### Margaret Thatcher and small talk
>
> *Margaret Thatcher would hate people asking how she was or talking about the weather, but talk politics and you saw the glint in her eye and she was off. I was standing in a line-up ready to greet Mrs Thatcher next to a Scottish friend. I politely greeted her with a handshake but he greeted her with a question that he was not sure she was right about the Community Charge; well, he put it a little more strongly than that! What felt like ten minutes later her aids were almost pulling her away from the brief, heated debate that had ensued.*

She was just not interested in passing the time of day in small talk. She saved her words for something that really mattered to her.

If someone is cold they will be more likely to give short, sharp answers than if they were comfortably sitting in their armchair by a warm fire. Even being around familiar surroundings will make you more comfortable for any questions that are to come.

If you want to influence someone then make sure they are well and comfortable. It is very difficult to ask the same question a second time once you have already been given an answer. Usually you only get one chance. Make it count.

The worldview that the responder has

As discussed in my earlier books our worldview sets up all our judgements and our decisions. Understanding someone's worldview is key in being able to work with, influence and get the results you need.

Although one way to understand a person's worldview is to ask questions there are many other ways. You can even get hints and tips from:

- what they are wearing;
- body language;
- what they are saying;
- how they are saying something;
- background research material through talking to others or social media;
- and of course asking questions too.

However you find out, it will mean you need to think differently about how you ask the question. Take the worldview of this gentleman:

> **A very different point of view**
>
> In the 1980s I worked for a retail head office, John Menzies Plc, overseeing the installation of computer systems in the UK nationwide stores. In those days managers were asked to take copies of their data with floppy disks, either 5 1/4 inches or 8 inches. Sorry if you were born after 1990; you probably do not remember these. Each store had a very clear written procedure for taking disk copies. On one occasion a manager said he had a problem with his system and to cut a long story short he needed to go to his back-up copies and restore the data to the previous day's data. I asked him to follow the procedure to restore the data. An hour later he called to say he could not put the copies in the machine. In the end, I realised that he had been copying the disks every night but his personal understanding of copying was putting them in the photocopier! Of course there was no way to recover the data and the whole database had to be rebuilt from information manually. Who now does not understand copying data? Consider that in 2018 there are still over 50,000 households with black and white televisions.
>
> This gentleman had either not read or understood the instructions and thus it was not part of his worldview. I suppose why should he read them!

I learned a long time ago that we sometimes expect too much from people. I have a good friend who is a Concorde pilot. If you asked me how to fly Concorde is it reasonable for me to know how? No! However, if you asked Alex how to fly Concorde he would obviously tell you with great passion.

I was working with a team to deliver leadership and management training in my twenties and whilst in the wings of the stage, waiting for my piece of this training day to come about, I monitored the body language of the audience regarding what they were hearing and thus receiving. I saw nothing but confusion! It dawned on me that the training level we were delivering was far above their current knowledge level. We had assumed they all knew the basics. Remember, never assume!!

> ### The Importance of etiquette
>
> *After understanding this I put together a leadership weekend for some younger leaders. As it was a weekend we deliberately had a formal black-tie dinner in the evening. One of the final sessions before dinner was to go through dinner etiquette. Then on the dinner tables, the name cards had etiquette reminders on the back. I was quite surprised at the reaction of offence and fury by 40% of those that attended and absolute congratulations from the other 60%. In a discussion the next day the 60% won the day and the 40% realised the same thing I had; we sometimes expect people to know more than they do. Would you know which side to take your roll from at a formal dinner?*

The relationship between the questioner and the responder

Everyone is different and we all know, when meeting people for the first time, whether we are going to get on well or not. Part of this is trust. It is a powerful motivator and provides a great grounding for questions being answered honestly. In many cases, we are all a little sceptical of why people are asking questions. You need the person to whom you are asking the questions, to trust you. How are you going to achieve that?

I personally go through a process of tree mapping in my mind possible reasons someone is asking a question of me. This is no longer conscious but an automatic process. I essentially do it so that I can help them get to their real answer more quickly.

> **Star Wars**
>
> *I knew my son of twelve desperately wanted to go and see the latest Star Wars movie at the cinema as he had been going on about it for some weeks and so when, out of the blue, he asked was I free on Sunday afternoon I answered "Yes, we can go and see Star Wars at the cinema".*

I am sure we have all done this.

It was not the answer to the question he asked about being free on Sunday! It was the answer to the question he really wanted to ask and so I helped him get to the right answer by anticipating the question.

The relationship between the questioner and responder needs to be drawn out and discussed

Every person is different in the way they receive communication and the way they process what they have heard. Much of this comes from their own worldview but the difference in a person needs to be taken into account when asking questions.

The responder might be:

- a nervous person;
- a confident person;
- a shy person;
- a naturally defensive person;
- an arrogant person.

How will they best receive a question?

Culture and questions

I have worked with and in different countries and during that time it was clear from the start that there were very different cultures involved. Upon learning this I often specifically instructed my team as to how they were to handle some of the first encounters and that set the scene for some very productive relationships which helped both sides.

Say what you mean is our culture

We carried out a wash-up from a large programme which involved English, Scottish and German teams. The Germans fed back some important information to the English and Scottish team members.

Why are you so polite when you ask for something? You say, "It would be really good if you could get that done by Friday" and when Friday comes and we have not done it we realise you meant it must be done by Friday. Why did you not just say that in the first place?

The White House

In my younger days, I was a delegate for a briefing in The White House Washington. There was also a Japanese delegation and in our discussions, prior to the briefing, they were very much in agreement with our stance on many of the issues. Each time we discussed it they nodded their head in agreement... You are probably already ahead of me... In the meeting they completely reversed their positions and blindsided us. It was only later I realised that a nod meant they had heard what we had said, not that they agreed with us.

Even our normal talking speed and that of other nations is usually too fast when you are involving second-language representatives. Part of any first international meeting I convene is to set the ground rules on how we are going to communicate.

I slow the talking down considerably and insist that key messages are summarised by both sides. This means those key messages are played back to me and, in my experience, this leads to a higher probability of understanding.

There are still occasions within some cultures when someone will say what they think you want to hear and do something completely different. This is the challenge of working with different people and different teams.

If a person is abrupt and quick to action they really do not want someone going around the houses in the discussion. Go straight to the point and ask outright.

If the person needs convincing of something and is a detail person then give them the detail before getting to the question.

You, as a questioner, have a type as well. If your normal approach is abrupt then realise what that can do to the responder. They may become instantly defensive!

Consider these examples. Questions can be asked:

- aggressively or calmly;
- in an over bearing manner;
- in an interested or bored way;
- in a light-hearted, joking manner;
- in a severe, serious manner.

How do you ask your questions and do you adapt?

Consider how an aggressive approach to a question may be received by an aggressive person? It could make a situation volatile and might make them angry whereas a meek person might be intimidated.

You need to learn to adapt your own behaviour to suit the person who is going to be answering your questions. That may be just to change your body language. It may be that you need to smile before you ask the question.

Try a long-winded detailed question with a military person and then ask the same question directly. Which has the best answer and which leaves the best impression? Then ask the same question to someone who has the view of a stereotypical civil servant. Sorry, civil servants, I know you are not all alike. I think you get my point. The ability to adapt your own personality is vital in getting the results you need.

This difference in responder is against a backdrop of you the questioner. The way you are feeling will have an impact; whether you had a good night's sleep and whether you are tired, grumpy, happy, attentive, short-tempered, etc.

As the questioner, you can change some of your own situations but you can also adapt if you are aware of the other person's traits and current status, but only if you are aware of them. To some degree, you can act a nervous type, a confident, shy, defensive, or arrogant type and this will all have an impact on the questioner/responder relationship and so the answers. All of this is the Immersed Questioning Environment and should be taken into account whenever questioning is carried out.

So there are different types of people and questions operating in a constantly shifting environment, but there are also different types of answers, different types of questions and different ways of asking questions and all done within that complex changing environment.

Who said questioning was easy!

It is said within the English language, especially, that the way you deliver the same words can have completely different meanings. Well, the same can be said for the way questions are answered.

CHAPTER 5

THE CONSTITUENTS OF QUESTIONING

The constituents of questions and questioning can be broken down into three parts: style, content and delivery.

Whilst these overlap the analysis of each of them will help a person understand how the approach to designing questions and questioning can improve.

The style is about the type of question that is being asked. How you put the question together. The way the language is put together. It may be as simple as whether they are short or long questions or questions with an aggressive or passive tone. It may be the tense that is used. Each different type of question will usually achieve a different outcome and will be explored in this section.

Content is the actual words that are used instead of whether the questions themselves are long or short. It can include the length of the individual words, though. Are the words long or short, complicated or easy?

> **Literacy in the UK**
>
> The OECD study of basic skills in 2017 ranked England as the lowest country in literacy and second lowest in numeracy in the developed world. It is accepted that 1,000 words are used in day-to-day language by the majority of people. This means that some people either do not have 1,000 words in their vocabulary or they do not understand elementary grammar. In fact the literacy test is not even 1,000 words. Questioning must therefore take this into account.

In my experience content is often more complicated than it needs to be. It is important to keep questions very simple and the words as short as possible. When you deviate from this ensure that those receiving the question will be comfortable with it and able to understand it.

Finally, questioning requires delivery. This can be the medium used (written or verbal, email, letter, one-to-one, group) but can also include the way it is delivered.

The delivery mechanism should never be taken for granted. I have seen the most horrific escalation of a problem because someone used an exclamation mark. Do you know how to use one? It may be fine but beware, if the person you are sending the question to does not it can lead to terrible misunderstandings.

> **Clash Royale**
>
> *I spent a little time with my children (well, that is my excuse) playing Clash Royale, an online game. I got quite offended with some of the very short comments that were given to me by my opponent after I finished the game or during the game. If you lose and someone clicks on a "Good game!", how do you react? If you make a mistake and someone clicks on "Well played", how do you feel? I spoke with some other players who said they did it genuinely to congratulate the player. It was never about upsetting them. Didn't work with me! Probably because I kept losing!*

Since around 2017 I have started to receive so many more texts and WhatsApp messages!

These are short messages which are often sent to the wrong person, easily done, and for me can be taken so many different ways with little or no feedback.

> **Not a word to use on texts**
>
> *On a trip back from Cyprus in 2017 I sent a message to my wife saying I was going to need to shut down as the aeroplane was about to push back.*
>
> *To my horror spellcheck had changed one letter of the word shut down! The u was replaced with an i. Not a word I would normally use. I am sure this has happened to us all.*

Consider the medium you use and if at all possible try to use a medium that allows instant visible feedback.

Style

There are many different styles of questioning:

- simple question and answer;
- comparative questions;
- multiple questions;
- creative questions;
- leading questions;
- action questions;
- summarising questions;
- rhetorical questions;
- analysing and probing questions.

In exploring the different styles they can often be mixed, matched and used together to form a specific style.

Simple question and answer

A simple question and answer question is a question that is asked only for the answer. There are a number of types of simple question and answer questions which solicit different responses and are used in the formation of a number of the styles of questions in this chapter.

Closed questions/direct questions

A closed question is an example of a simple question. The definition of a closed question is a question which can be answered with a single word or short phrase.

Closed questions usually solicit a simple yes or no answer, but, if not yes or no they will always expect a simple word or two. Occasionally someone may use what I call a flip word like probably or maybe. Generally, if you are asking a closed question you need to insist on a closed, short one-word answer.

This very popular type of question is short, sharp and simple and this can be very useful for what I call convergent thinking, for closing down situations, for clarity and getting to the end point.

There should be no ambiguity in a closed question. Do you think global warming is a real threat? Yes or no. Do not allow maybe! Maybe solicits a follow-up question which is likely to be an open question.

Closed and direct types of questions are often used in cross-examination in courts, as they are very effective at leaving control with the questioner.

Although many just consider closed questions to be a yes or no question, closed questioning can deviate from yes or no. For instance, "So would you like the blue or green car?". This is a conditional close in selling and demands one of two answers. Blue or green. What happened to black or white or blue with a racing stripe over the top? The questioner has led the responder. A tip for later in the book when we look at answers is when answering questions why do you need to agree the conditions or assumptions in the question? A sales agent will still be delighted if you say "What happened to yellow?", not one of the options, but they have still taken you to the next stage, subconsciously agreeing to buy if you can have yellow.

Some people also state that direct answers are more truthful but realistically deception can still occur in a trained individual.

Closed questions can be used to help the questioner be more sure of something and confirm that you have it absolutely right. So "Is blue the only colour you have available?". It is clear that if "yes" is stated and subsequently found to be untrue then the person must have been mistaken or deliberately attempting to mislead.

So direct or closed questions are often shorter and to the point and, as all questions, always contain a question mark.

Direct questions will use words like:

- If…
- Do…
- Will…
- Would…
- Are…
- Can…

at the beginning of the actual question.

Use direct questions to leave no ambiguity. Use them for convergent thinking for closing down and confirming knowledge.

Indirect/open questions
Now as opposed to direct or closed questions the opposite is true for indirect and open questions which allow for divergent thinking. Divergent thinking is so much more creative.

These questions will receive a much longer answer. If your objective is to find out someone's view or just to get them talking, then open questions are the right approach. Indirect questions will also help to improve relationships or just get further information.

Look at this example of a closed and open question for the same subject:

An example might be "Are you going out tonight?". This is a yes/no answer whereas "Where are you going tonight?" is more open and will give you further information. It will confirm the answer to the direct question as to whether the person is going out tonight.

One downside of open questions is that clear information is not always provided and irrelevant information can be given which will need to be sifted through. Information presented is also likely to be very biased to the responder's worldview.

Open questions do, however, allow you to learn more and are a vital source for building the PKB, Personal Knowledge Base.

Open questions do not only solicit a person's opinion on things but also how they feel, and are likely to help in understanding their values and drivers.

Where closed questions keep control with the questioner, open questions relinquish considerable control to the responder as they can take the dialogue in any direction the responder wishes.

Again these types of questions make up the styles discussed later in the chapter but almost always start with words like why and how.

- Why do you think…?
- How does that work…?
- What do you think about…?

Comparative questions
Comparative questioning is where a question or series of questions are comparing two or more variables. It is looking to understand the difference between these variables.

A comparative question may, therefore, start with "What is the difference between… (the variables)?". It might also be a little more disguised. Well, there is… variable… and… variable… What do you think about them? What tells them apart?

For example:

- What is the difference between men and women?
- What is the difference in the hearing of men and women?
- Why is swimming more exciting than running?

Comparative questions can also be used as leading questions as you are limiting the comparison to the variables you set out. In the above question it is swimming and running. What about basketball? This is similar to our conditional close-in closed questions. However, the difference is the comparison between the two variables.

Research has also shown that different answers will be given depending upon which variable is in which position. So, in the example above, swimming is before running and therefore more people would opt for swimming as being more exciting than running. This is another way of leading a responder. Once someone says something then it can be subconsciously accepted even if the person would normally not have agreed to it.

If they write it down, then it becomes even more powerful but that is another book!

Multiple questions
Multiple questions are questions that have more than one question built in. This can be seen in any walk of life but is often seen where people are only allowed to ask one question.

Can you tell me who it was that leaked that document and by what means? This is clearly two questions, one to solicit the who and the other to find the medium they used to leak it.

How much additional cash will you put into the NHS and how will it be spent differently?

These are clearly two different questions in the same question.

A good structured multiple question can allow one to lead onto the other. Take the NHS answer to a politician. It is likely that they will be able to quote the answer to how much and so it is very powerful to link the cash with how it is going to be spent, something they usually cannot or do not wish to answer.

It is not, however, impossible to have a multiple question with no link between the two questions. The questioner might just concatenate them. Is the nuclear deterrent safe and can you tell me how much we raised in taxes last year?

Multiple questions have their place but unless leading the questioner then why not simply ask the two questions separately? This will allow a change to the second question if the answer is not what was expected from the first question.

Take the example about the NHS. There is no extra cash. The second question is now redundant.

Creative questions
Creative questioning is again a divergent questioning format. It opens up to new ideas and allows people to create ideas and concepts. It is often defined as a variant of open and indirect questioning.

I often use this style of questioning in my Directive Coaching. Directive Coaching was expanded on in an earlier chapter.

- How would you react if… happened?
- What would it be like if…?
- How would it be different if…?
- Suppose that…?
- What would change if…?

- Why do you think…?
- How would it look differently if…?

Creative questioning is not necessarily about expecting to find a solution but leading clear, divergent thinking.

It might be creating a story, a picture, an abstract. There does not need to be an end and the only objective may be the action of creatively thinking and exploring itself.

Creative questioning can help with understanding possibilities, parameters, size of something and can even be just for fun. It can also help explore the holistic picture before deciding upon the avenues to expand further.

Creative questioning also has a place in reflecting on a person, a situation or something specific.

Creative questioning can include:

- Substituting
- Changing
- Modifying
- Removing
- Flipping
- Adapting
- Combining
- Composing
- Designing
- Creating
- Inventing
- Visualising

an item or an idea.

So questions may contain the starting words:

- Visualise this…
- Design…
- Invent…
- Extrapolate this…
- Compose…
- Discuss…
- Hypothesise…
- Compare and contrast…
- Transform…

These verbs added into a question will enable creative questioning.

As AI (Artificial Intelligence) becomes more and more a part of our lives, creative thinking and creative questioning will become more and more important to the human condition. Some would disagree but it is a key component humans have over machines.

Leading questions
Almost every form of questioning can be used to lead the responder or indeed others listening to the responder. Journalists use this to great effect.

There is a saying that there is no smoke without fire and I know this can be completely untrue.

> **The box in the corner**
>
> One of my first trades was electronic and computer engineering.
>
> I was also involved in politics. In one of our elections a newspaper was informed that someone had planted a bug in a hotel room in Manchester at a meeting of the opposing group in the election and that this was a dirty trick. The other team went as far as informing the police and, of course, leaked it to the press. It appeared in the newspaper the next day with a profile which fitted me exactly! However, at no time did they mention my name as planting it. The police investigated and said a black box with a wire leading from it had been found in the room. No electronics, nothing and yet there was no retraction from the group or newspaper. The damage to the election campaign had been done. My team was seen as the bad team but we, and specifically I, had done nothing wrong. These were the dirty tricks carried out by the other side. Where is the smoke without fire there!

From a questioning point of view this story is to reinforce to you that once a subject has been raised individuals commit it to their subconscious and the picture they have committed is very difficult to remove, even if there has been a retraction.

Leading questions, however, should be used cautiously. Please make sure you are doing it for the right reasons.

Leading questions can also be asked with an assumption. You may have a hunch or are working on a hypothesis. How much over budget will your project be? (Who said the project would be over budget? You are making the assumption that it will be.) Remember, when answering a question, you can always deny an assumption but do it rigorously and immediately. Provide facts to back up the denial.

So if you approach a project manager and question them about their project being over budget they may state it is not, even if it is going to be, because they will naturally become defensive, and I would suggest your relationship will not be enhanced.

> ### *"The Affair"*
>
> At my lighting company I suspected a staff member was having a relationship with her boss, who worked for me. Now I see nothing wrong with that per se, but my view was that the situation needed to be openly acknowledged because at that time it was already causing some talk within the factory.
>
> One morning I stated vaguely that "one should be careful where one leaves their car overnight, especially in streets such as…"; the manager's location was included. Now, this was a question levelled as a statement to solicit an answer. The answer came back "No! Did you see it?". To which I answered "See what?" and I had a pouring out of the truth. The relationship was out in the open and my objective was achieved. Subsequently, they married each other and the issue resolved itself. Everyone knew where they stood and felt they could talk more openly.

Adding your own personal view, in the phrasing of a question, is also considered to be leading questioning. "The dress is available in green or white. Isn't green nice?" You did not mention it was also available in other colours and you suggested green was the best! Your view or the customers? This is very much leading people and narrowing down options. It is also used in sales as it assumes you are going to pick one of them. There is suggestion that you are going to buy. It is called the presumptive close.

Leading questions can also be those that indicate an action or drive a command: "You are going to stay up to take my call. Yes?"

Leading can also tie in with the "yes preference" as I call it. We all like to say yes rather than no, well, most of us. So when a question is put it is often phrased to get the answer the questioner wants with a yes. Journalists are trained to use this technique. The question "So is that the first time you have done it?" will most likely solicit a yes but it can be rephrased as "So that isn't the first time you have done it, is it?"

> ### The trainee politician
>
> Andy, acting as an interviewer in a training session, used this leading questioning technique to get continual yes answers and a particular future politician was so confused by the way the questions were asked, he said yes to the comment "So you are saying that Margaret Thatcher should bomb Russia?" Seconds after, he realised what he had said and retracted the comment but the sound bite was already canned and ready to go to air, if it had been a real event.

Leading questions can get you your own way whilst bringing people with you. They are not always used for bad. It comes back to one of my central themes. What is the objective of your questioning? Something we will explore further with the Advanced Power Questioning Framework.

Action question

Questions for action are often considered leading questions but they do not have to be. They are questions that raise a call for action. They will always have a verb in the question such as:

- Make – Will you make me a cake for my birthday, please?
- Take – Can you take me to the station, please?
- Give – Are you able to give me a summary today?

Questions such as:

- Will you deliver the food, please?
- Can you buy the tickets, please?
- Can you please look up the weather today?

The call to action can be explicit or implicit. That is it may be very clearly stated or it may be something that you realise needs to be done by reading the question (implicit). For instance, "Is it possible to challenge the planning permission?"

Summarising

A summarising question is simply a question which summarises either a position, or some other detail within the question.

"So we have to spend £150 on the ski pass whether we go skiing or not?" I would suggest the objective of this question might be to inform the person about the cost of the ski pass as well, but either way the question is summarised.

A summarising question is thus a question that plays back information. This might be by paraphrasing information within the question.

"So are you saying the performance is not as good because the petrol is inferior and the catalytic converter is also malfunctioning?" It is a question but summarises the information already presented.

Summarising questions are incredibly powerful for checking understanding from all parties and for imparting information without appearing too dictatorial and this is vital in communicating for success.

Rhetorical questions

Are these questions? Are they statements? I've put them in the category of questions. They may not elicit an answer externally or in a conventionally understood questioning way but they usually achieve an objective by asking a question; often a question that will be influencing someone or leading them.

It may not even be external but internally rhetorical questions may help you appreciate something, understand something, clarify something or just plain make you feel better. They still form part of questioning.

Rhetorical questioning can be open, closed, direct, analysing. In fact, it can be any type of question but not necessarily one that is expecting an answer.

Analysing and probing questions

Analysing and probing questions are probably the most used questions and there are a number of different types. These questions dig further, explore, enquire and can even interrogate. It is divergent, but also an exploratory style of questioning that is about uncovering facts, discovering things and taking ideas further.

These are some of the different types of analysing and probing questions.

Probing questions

Probing questions can get the responder to open up on a particular topic. It is often as easy as getting them to run through an example, probing more into the detail and being interested in understanding the answer a little more.

Clarifying information probing questions will use techniques such as the Kipling technique or the five whys. These are covered later in this chapter.

Cross-examination questions

Cross-examination is usually done in a very assertive manner. The whole point is to try to understand whether there is truth and so will always be threatening to a degree.

Cross-examination is also definitely classified under leading questions. In fact, it is probably the most obvious type of probing question you come across.

When you cross-examine your aim is to tell an individual what to say, but of course, that is not possible. However, with questioning you can lead them to the point they are just answering closed and leading questions allowing you to remain in control.

"So this knife is owned by you?" This is very different from "Do you know who owns this knife?".

Questions such as why and how are never used. Short, simple, closed questions work the best with only yes or no answers possible.

In cross-examination your aim is also to tell a story by leading a witness through the story but it is imperative that it is done one simple step at a time. Additionally using steps that are backed up with fact and evidence always helps.

So each question will just have one point and will often be staged to finish with "Do you agree?" or "Is it not true?". In the end these short post-question clarifications can be removed. "So the time of the dinner was 5pm. Do you agree?" This becomes "The time of the dinner was 5pm, yes?". There you have given them the answer. All they now need to do is confirm it and people generally prefer to agree than disagree with others.

A cross-examination question is built to get the required answer providing no room to manoeuvre. If you phrase the question to ensure as much of the fact is at the end of your question with a "right?" inserted it will increase the pressure on the witness as it leaves them less time to think.

It is not only the yes/no answer that defines interrogative questioning but often the tone which is used that defines the "interrogative mood" that is set. The tone, often with a rise in intonation at the end, will change a sentence to become interrogative. When added to the more formal surroundings it will feel interrogative to the responder even if it is not supposed to be the case.

The final advice on cross-examination is to use plenty of questions to build your story, step by step. Do not try to "boil the ocean" with multiple questions.

The use of questioning in analysis
Another form of probing question can be called diagnostic questioning. This is a type of question which is going to try to improve understanding or break things down further, perhaps working through to the cause. As before it may call upon types of questioning such as open and closed types. Diagnostic questioning is usually very focused.

A problem-solving framework will be introduced later in Section III.

Explorative questioning is another type of probing question. It still tends to follow the same principles as the other analysis questions and questioning. Here open and indirect questions will allow more information to be presented. It is the questioner who needs to keep on track to where you want or need to explore.

Do not allow the responder to let the answers to these inquiring questions drift. Practise your line of questioning and be clear where you think you want to go, and keep your wits about you if things take you in a direction you were not expecting but remains relevant.

Always consider pausing and rethink your questions if you find they are not achieving your purpose.

These inquiring questions can often have follow-up after follow-up which will help you analyse a situation.

As opposed to interrogative questioning these types of questions need people to give as much as they can in a divergent mode and so this should never be carried out in a threatening way. You will always come up short if you make people perceive the questioning to be a threat.

The content of questions

It is widely recognised that there are around 600,000 words in the English language although this is not exact as many words have different meanings and so officially no exact number has been declared by the Oxford English Dictionary. Out of those 600,000 words it is accepted by non-English first language speakers that 1,000 words will achieve between 80-90% of your needs and other experts declare that 90-95% of your language needs are around 3,000 words!

Thus the use of the words you use must be clearly aligned with your target audience. If you use really long words or rare words to a non-English first language speaker then they will probably not understand your question, but many other people will.

It is unlikely your objective in questioning is to impress people with your language skills and so I teach "Keep it Simple, Silly" (KISS) as a technique.

This book is not designed to be a book on English and so this is a short section. However, I recommend you to source a book on the English language itself. There has been a proliferation of books written through the centuries.

Knowing English language and having a good grasp of the grammar of the language will help put the content of a question together in a way that optimises the likelihood of achieving your objective.

If the technicalities of the English language are a weak area for you then it would be wise to learn more about them.

It will certainly make using the content for questioning much easier.

So learn how to put together words so they make sense.

How to, and when to, use smaller words or longer words.

How to use:

- Verbs
- Nouns
- Adjectives
- Adverbs
- Conjunctions
- Prepositions
- Pronouns

all to create the ideal question.

Remember to align the level to apply the right words for the person who has to answer.

Delivery

The delivery media a question is delivered by can be just as important as the way it is constructed and the content. There have been stories where companies have "fired" people by text. The outrage is quite justified. It is therefore important in questioning to consider the right delivery method for the questioning to ensure you meet your objective of the questioning.

The best medium for delivery can be influenced by:

- the purpose/objective;
- the type of content;
- the other person's preference;
- the time and cost;
- physical constraints such as distance;
- also how and if you require feedback.

If you require immediate feedback this may exclude the medium of email, for example, but might include the telephone.

The preparation and planning that goes into the content and style should be done knowing the delivery medium, if at all possible, as it might change both the content and style.

However, all the preparation and planning may be wasted if the delivery is not done well. The delivery often secures the results.

I have been teaching people different techniques in presentation and delivery for over thirty-five years and this could be the subject for a complete book as well. Therefore, once again I represent the topic here as more of an overview of how it relates to questioning.

Methods of delivery

Verbal:

- Face to face; either one to one, many to many or many to one.
- Third-party conversation where you and I are in a group talking to each other. This could be included in face to face.
- Gossip. This again can be done face to face or through written forms. However, worth mentioning as it is so powerful.
- A message through someone else, often referred to as a proxy.
- Through television or some media representation such as an app or teleconferencing.
- Telephone, whether video or audio. Remember pure audio loses important body language.
- Radio or some other audio-only medium.

In written form:

- Memo
- Letter
- Email
- Internet
- Specific peer-to-peer app
- Peer-to-many app
- This can include social media

Each form of delivery has its place in questioning, depending upon what you are trying to achieve. However, sometimes you have no choice but to use a certain form of delivery mode and indeed you may need to allow for two different methods at the same time. For instance you may need to submit the written question and then have to verbalise it to actually deliver it.

Verbal delivery
With verbal delivery, the questioner must consider the speed of delivery.

How fast are you going to talk? Most people talk at between 140 and 160 words a minute but if nervous this can be even faster. If you are talking to someone where English is not their first language then it needs to be slowed down to 110 words a minute. It may also need to be slowed down for a child or an elderly person or someone with impaired hearing.

The tone of delivery
The tone may also solicit a different response.

- Angry tone
- Gentle tone

Even just smiling when on a telephone and talking to someone will soften the tone of the delivery. There are so many salespeople who deliberately stand when they are talking to customers because it gives a much better impression, a dynamic impression, on the other end of the phone and so always consider posture.

The volume of delivery
How much are you actually going to say? Think about this and try to keep it as short as possible.

Gestures
The gestures that are used as part of the delivery.

Gestures are part of body language and that is thought to be over 65% of communication. Choose your gestures carefully. Are they to be:

- Threatening?
- Strong?
- Weak?

The use of pauses

For many years I have taught people to present. The careful use of the "pause" can completely change the meaning of a sentence and if not change the meaning allow focus on particular areas subconsciously as well as consciously.

It is also well recognised that people fill silences. I personally do not have an issue with silence and often will let the silence remain preferring the other party to talk and show their hand. Do you need to use pauses, or could you use pauses to achieve a better response to the questions you ask?

Clarity in delivery

There are different types of people and different approaches for each type of person. Consider being:

- blunt and to the point;
- indirect; or even
- verbose.

The delivery of a verbal question can be affected by just a difference in the positive approach to that question.

Body language

Your body language and eye contact are critical when asking questions. Are they aligned with the question you are asking? If you are asking in a hostile way is your body language showing the hostility needed to carry it off? Does it mean a little bit of "acting"? Personally, I would not say acting but adapting to the situation.

What happens if you say something:

- With a cold feeling?
- In a reflective style?
- In a conversational style or casual style?
- In an analytical style?
- In a dramatic way?
- In an emotional way?
- In a positive or negative way?

Also the real understanding of the question asked; has the meaning been transmitted and received correctly. With verbal the answer can be immediately validated. The responder can be asked to summarise the message sent and thus confirm that it was received correctly.

Verbal questions in an international environment
I have done a number of years of international work in both Germany and Italy. It became very clear, very quickly, that there were always misunderstandings between the different teams within the countries. I therefore set up a process of ensuring that clear feedback and summary was given at regular intervals. I would also go away, summarise, and later represent the summary to the parties to ensure these misunderstandings were minimised. I also ensured that all parties spoke at a much slower than usual speed.

Just remember when you deliver questions verbally there are three versions:

- the one you planned;
- the one you delivered; and
- the one that was heard and interpreted.

You must be able to adapt which is a vital part of the delivery.

Written communications

A written question is similar to a verbal question and again one needs to consider the style and content. However, there is no opportunity to go back, if in written form, and clarify the question or follow the question with another question and so it needs to be considered on its own.

To manage this, the question will need to succinctly get to the point and may also need to be in a multiple questioning format. It will, therefore, need more care in the crafting and exploring of possible answers.

Go through and consider the top five answers you may get from the question. If those are not the likely answers you need then redraft the question. It is usual that you get more time to prepare a written question.

The written communication can still be done in the same way as a verbal question:

- with a cold feel;
- a reflective style;
- a conversational style or casual style;
- an analytical style;
- with dramatic prose;
- an emotional pull on the reader;
- positively and negatively.

Written communication does have an advantage in that it is more likely to be "on record", another reason for making sure it is right from the start. There is also no need for personal contact and this may be an advantage.

In office situations, these advantages and disadvantages can be important and should be considered. My own question will always come back to what do you want to achieve and what is the best way of achieving it.

Advantages:

- greater preparation time is usually available and longer crafting is possible;
- it is a much more effective way of recording what was asked and the following answer;
- there is less chance that there can be a denial of the question being asked and indeed the content of the question;
- it is more often private; and
- there is no need for personal contact.

Disadvantages:

- it is not fast and is generally one way;
- it is only able to be read by those who can read the language in which it is written. In the UK that could drastically reduce the number of people able to read it (as has already been mentioned, literacy has declined in the last fifty years);
- it has a greater likelihood that it may be misinterpreted.

It is not as effective as verbal questioning as it is more difficult to adapt to the responder based on body language, or any other type of feedback. Also, the power of verbal communication includes so many other factors described in the verbal section such as pauses, tone, volume and body language. There is no body language in a written question.

Section III

CHAPTER 6

ANSWERING QUESTIONS

Answering questions in an effective way

There have been many, many times when the way a CEO has addressed a crisis has decided their fate.

In 2015 the CEO of Volkswagen quickly apologised for a deliberate breach of emissions compliance with a sophisticated software routine added to some cars to understand when an emissions "compliance test" was being carried out. It was clear from day one that the public and regulators were not totally convinced with the way the apology was given. Some people doubted the honesty and that resulted very rapidly in his resignation.

> **Vox Pops**
>
> *Throughout my time in politics, I would often have a television camera thrust in my face and a question asked. The news crews were always looking for something controversial. Something that would excite their audiences. It became a real skill to decide whether you wanted your clip to be used, and believe it or not that was often within your control. If you stayed on message it was unlikely the clip would be used but if you said something of "interest", something "controversial" then it was likely to be aired on the six, seven, eight, nine and ten o'clock news.*

As many politicians, leaders and executives will know questioning is important but answering questions effectively is just as important.

There are techniques which you can use in providing answers and a number of these are explored here.

Firstly, it may seem silly, but listen to the question. If you did not hear it or need further time to think, ask for it to be repeated.

Consider the question – the pause is so powerful and yet people feel uncomfortable with it. Don't be. Those that ask the questions understand and appreciate that you are giving worthwhile consideration to their question.

During the pause ask yourself:

- What does the question actually mean?
- What is the person trying to get from the question?
- Is there a trap and how do you avoid falling into it?
- Do you want to answer the question?

- Is it a question you are compelled to answer? And why?
- Is it generally a leading question?
- Do you mind being led?
- Is it a leading question that will cause you to confirm an assumption in the question?

> ### *Yes, prime minister*
>
> *The famous saying from the BBC's "Yes, Prime Minister" comes to mind where Sir Humphrey tells his aid, Bernard: "If you have nothing to say, say nothing. But better, have something to say and say it, no matter what they ask. Pay no attention to the question, make your own statement. If they ask you the same question again, you just say, that's not the question or I think the more important question is this... Then you make another statement of your own. Easy-peasy."*

Personally, I recommend you always try to answer the question if you can.

> ### *Sky News – Margaret Thatcher*
>
> *I was interviewed live on "Morning Break" Sky News back in November 1991 on the subject of Margaret Thatcher's re-election for the Conservative leadership and prime minister. That was the morning that Margaret resigned but at 8.20am the fight was still on.*
>
> *I was being interviewed along with a federal European supporter about the current situation with the Conservative Party. I was questioned about a number of different things but I needed to get the subject off Mrs Thatcher and back onto the reason for the attack on Mrs Thatcher. This was a march*

> towards a federal Europe which she did not support. The real story was about a possible resignation, and despite being asked the question about Mrs Thatcher resigning, I did the classic reply… "Well, that is not the question. The question is whether we should be going towards a Federalist Europe" which the interviewer promptly picked up and questioned the Federal supporter next to me. His response gave the message I needed to give to the population which was a weak response taking us off the fragile subject of a resignation. Mrs Thatcher resigned some two hours later.

Driving the message or communication you want to give is important. Consider when providing the answer the propensity to have things used out of context and for people to not listen properly and so miss things. I will rarely allow the use of pronouns, or the reply of a non-descript organisation, in answers to me.

The use of pronouns

Time and time again people will say "they do not like this". This response is not acceptable. I want to know who does not like it. Name names and do not use pronouns. If someone states something or asks a question with a pronoun such as we, she, he or they, I will take them to task. Who is we? Who are they? This protects from great misunderstandings and of course hiding behind the "business or organisation". It is almost never an organisation, it is an individual. Seek out the individual.

If you are the one answering the questions don't hide behind them either.

"The business wants this – no, who in the business wants it?"

> ### It's on its way
>
> I ran an electronics manufacturing company for eleven years and one day I needed some key components for a customer order. I phoned my supplier who said the order was on its way to me by them. I asked who "they" were and was told. I subsequently asked for the tracking number. It was at that point they said it was in the warehouse and had not been put on the van yet. I asked at what point did it arrive at the warehouse. A short delay and I was told it was with customs at the port. I asked for the customs document number. A further short delay; it was in transit from Singapore. I asked for the transit number and was told it had not left Singapore yet. All they needed to say was it was not yet available. I had to source those critical components from somewhere else but if I had not kept asking the questions taking out the "we", "they", "them", etc., I would have been delayed by days and missed our company's deadline.

Pronouns lead to assumptions and ambiguity. They can also show up anyone making an excuse or inventing a situation that really does not exist.

What is the reason for the question?

When answering questions it is unlikely that someone is trying to trap you, but it can happen. It is definitely something to be aware of if you suspect someone has had media training.

When answering a question work out the reason someone is asking the question.

Is it to:

- genuinely find out something;
- lead you to do something or think something;
- make a call to action in what they are asking;
- seek out the truth;
- ask a rhetorical question;
- really find the answer;
- trap you into saying something?

Advertising is awful but we still do it

I worked for a Sky PLC, a broadcasting company, and I was asked a question stating that adverts were awful and when was I going to get rid of them. "Nobody likes adverts!" the questioner went on to say. Now the short answer was we were not going to get rid of adverts as they provided a considerable income to the company but I was not going to achieve the right message saying that. So I ruled out the assumption that most people hate adverts. It is a clear assumption. My answer was that most people do not hate adverts, but admitted they only like adverts they are interested in and that are relevant to them. If you are interested in fast cars an advert about the latest fast car will be sure to have you watching it. So my approach was to identify what we were doing to ensure that adverts were more targeted. I went on to discuss how our current products were improving this targeting.

When you are giving an answer make sure it is the message you want to deliver which may not necessarily be the answer the questioner would like you to give. Consider carefully before you make it, or whether you make one at all; whether you are going to make it a qualified answer, one that has strings attached.

I have a technique I use when listening to people. Sometimes I keep quiet when someone has already answered the question. The responder often takes this to be because they need to provide more detail. It is often this additional information where I find the answers I need. The information that someone thought they would not give up initially.

I also watch for specific words that are often used to qualify something or even completely change something, turn it on its head, words such as maybe, possibly, could, might, but, etc.

Go through a day and count how many times these words are used. You will be surprised.

Positivity is key

If you want to impress someone when being interviewed you must be positive.

People tend to think more highly of you if you have a positive response. One example: If you talk to a child they will often give a naturally positive answer.

> ### How are you getting on with your music grades?
>
> *I once asked this of a young person and the immediate answer was "Well, I don't practise enough"! A better response might be, I am currently on target for the grade but I know if I want to move quickly to the next stage I will have to practise more. Both are true but the latter, a better, more positive answer.*

Frame the question to elicit the response you need.

Achieve your objective in answering

Ensure the message you communicate and is received is the message the questioner wants you to communicate.

What are your objectives? What do you want to communicate? This applies to a questioner and a responder. Here we are dealing with the responder so:

Make sure you have a good idea of what you are trying to achieve. Then answer it accordingly.

Let's go back to the concept, as with the questioner questioning: when I first hear a question my first thought always returns to that five-finger rule, that is to list five reasons they could be asking the question. What is their goal?

This not only helps me understand whether there is a trick in play but also if they are trying to lead me. Where are they trying to lead me to? And why are they trying to lead me?

And do I mind being led? Can I help them achieve their goal by being led? Can I achieve my goal by being led?

CHAPTER 7
AVOIDING QUESTIONS WHEN ANSWERING

There are times when you may need or want to avoid answering a question. This might be down to a legal or moral directive. It may be a banned or forbidden subject.

Questions that cover someone's looks or private subjects may be out of bounds. Politics and religion are often subjects people cannot or will not answer questions on. For instance a police officer is not allowed to get involved in party politics.

> ***Are you pregnant?***
>
> When I was about twenty-two I was at a reception talking to another gentleman and a young lady. A fourth person joined the group and his immediate question to the lady was "Are you pregnant?"! To which the lady responded "No, just fat". The question was inappropriate at that time and still would be today.

Take care when asking questions but feel free to respond with a knock-out blow if an inappropriate question is asked.

> ### The pension
>
> *My involvement in politics took me to many public meetings and on one occasion the speaker, Andrew, who was also a candidate for an upcoming election, was asked to comment about the pension issues coming up in the next ten to twenty years. This was a televised event and clearly, the government and this candidate knew there were issues but could not share these in a public meeting. The candidate stood up as if to answer the question but asked the questioner "Where did you get your information?". The questioner replied "The Daily Sun", an English newspaper. A good part of the audience started to laugh and the speaker replied, "Well, I think you have your answer…" And sat down. The question was a great question which was never answered.*

Do not get pressured into always having to answer the question.

I don't know

"I don't know the answer" can be really truthful and build trust. Now obviously if there is a reasonable expectation that you should know the answer this is probably not the best approach. However, you cannot know everything in life so sometimes the response "I don't know but will find out" may be the right answer. Perhaps follow up with "Could you leave your details and I will get back to you?". Possibly as many as nine times out of ten the person will never leave their details.

These days this honesty is much more accepted than saying something dishonest and nowadays bluffing through is so much more difficult as people have recording equipment or can uplink your answers in real time on Facebook or Twitter. If you don't know the answer say you don't know. The worst that will happen is that you will get criticised for not knowing. However, lie and your damage will not be limited to just that information. It could possibly include a loss of trust which is much harder to rebuild.

There is a process in the House of Commons which is talking out a debate so that they can prevent a vote being taken. This is called filibustering, However, a similar approach can be to say, "I will be answering that later in the presentation" or "Can we take that at the end?". The meeting often forgets the question or time runs out, especially, if you are in a meeting where the chair is on your side and happy to let it slide.

Answering the question you want to

Take a leaf out of Humphrey Appleby's book (BBC series *Yes Minister!*).

The primary way to avoid questions you do not want to answer is to make sure you know the questions you do want to answer and then answer only those questions.

So "Is Brexit good for Britain?". Your answer could be: "The European Union and the UK are working together on many different initiatives and this continues to be positive.". This could be your answer.

How is that answering the question? But you have answered a question and many people will not even spot you answered a completely different question. Now some interviewers will come back to it and ask it again. You again answer the question with different words but the same meaning.

Techniques in avoiding answering a question are:

The stall
Sometimes this means asking someone to repeat the question or clarify something whilst you have time to think about the answer you are going to give or can give.

Defer to someone else
Another approach is to defer to a more authoritative body. "I am not able to answer that question but 'so and so' is." The only thing is 'so and so' might not be too pleased.

Answer a different question to the one asked
Care needs to be taken here. If you do not answer the question it can appear evasive. If you answer a similar question to one that is asked or one that is in a related domain it is sometimes enough for an audience to not realise you have failed to answer the question. This was a technique I taught to politicians.

When you make a short speech, for instance, you go in with a maximum of three points to get across and no matter what is asked you need to get those three points across during the media time available. The same principle applies whether on stage or not but only give more if you really need to.

Define the scope up front and take control
Take control by telling everyone what subjects or issues you are prepared to answer questions on before the questions start. "I will now answer questions on…" This puts you in control and limits the exposure on what you are prepared to answer questions on.

Appear to answer the question
This is dangerous ground because you may well find that appearing to answer a question means you lead someone to believe you have said something that

you have not said and you may have to deny it later. More and more people will not accept those people who appear to answer the question and want to deny it later. The interpretation can be taken even if you imply the answer to the question and the "jury" will hold the implication as your answer anyway. This is more apparent nowadays with social media.

Answer the damn question
Why not!

A straight answer is usually the best. If at all possible, however, I often try to understand what goal someone has and try to help them towards the goal.

> *Play football*
>
> *"Is there any space on Saturday for Jonny to play football?" is a question that could be answered with "yes" or "no" but could say "I would be delighted to have Johnny join us". How is that answering the question that was asked? It is more likely answering the follow-up question. Of course, there is always risk on answering a question a person is asking because the questioner might have wanted to know if he could bring a Christmas present to hand over!! Luckily it was not the case on this occasion.*

A straight answer must be an honest and sincere answer. If you do answer honestly and sincerely you will be raised in the "I like you" factor, whether this is one to one or media.

Answer the question that they really want to ask
If you are a super confident person then you will be able to work through the reason for the question perhaps with the five-finger method described earlier. You may well be able to answer the question to which they are alluding. For

instance, What is your salary? is a question most people will not answer but is it really a question the person wants to ask or do they want to know how well people get paid relative to other companies. An answer "better than most people" in my line of work may be satisfactory.

There is, of course, the "No I am not going to answer that" question; care is needed with this approach as people become more inquisitive if there is a mystery involved.

Counter the question with a question

This can get incredibly frustrating and often does not work but an example like… "What are you doing this afternoon?" "What do you think I am doing?" "Oh, going to the shops." "Excellent, see you later then." Actually, there has been no definitive statement that they are going to the shops but the assumption is now that they are!

Only answer what you want or need to answer

Avoiding questions would not be complete without avoiding answering in more detail than you need to. Firstly make sure you really do understand the question and then decide whether you are going to give just a straight answer, or give additional information away as you give the answer. If it serves you to give additional information then do so. Otherwise do not.

For example:

Are you going out tonight? This is a yes/no answer. A closed question.

You could answer "Yes" and leave it like that but people like to talk and so they may say "Yes, between 7pm and 8pm". Both are truthful but one gives further information which technically was not requested. Does it matter? Sometimes it does and sometimes it doesn't. It really depends upon each unique situation and the objective of the questioner.

Declining to answer is sometimes more dangerous than answering as people love intrigue.

> ### A date with my girlfriend
>
> When I was twenty, before I was married, of course, I was planning a date. One of my friends really wanted to know what I was doing and where I was going and who I was going to meet. I declined to answer. This set up such an intrigue in his brain that he even followed me to find out what I was doing and where I was going. The lesson here is that being evasive is often not the best policy. Giving an outline will often be better than leaving the question "unanswered".

Challenge a person's right to ask the question

"I am sorry but who gives you the right to ask something that personal?" This is perfectly acceptable in the private world but may be an issue in the political world.

Answer the question before it is asked

There is a case to take the wind out of the sails for a question. That is to give the information in the way you want to before the question is asked.

Before trying to avoid or evade a question, though, why not just try to avoid landing yourself in situations in which you cannot answer questions.

Answer only one of the questions

If you want to avoid a question where someone has presented a multiple question you can always just answer the one you want to. Be careful and prepared that they may come back for a second bite at the second question.

Be briefed and prepared for questions

Who goes to a job interview without preparing for the likely questions?

I have given seminars and lectures all around the UK and one lesson I learned very early on is to be prepared. Think through your audience and the likely questions and tell them in advance if there are any real taboo questions. This can help reduce the embarrassment factor.

CHAPTER 8

HOW TO BECOME AN ADVANCED POWER QUESTIONER

How do you become a more effective questioner?

Questions exist almost everywhere we go and in almost everything we do. We rarely stop and think about the questions or how they are asked. We rarely reflect because we are busy getting answers ready in our own minds. Well, stop, think and analyse how someone is asking you a question. What are they asking? Try to work out their objective. Are they succeeding in their approach or what might be a better way?

Experiential learning is incredibly powerful. Learn by doing.

Take some examples of questions in your daily life and analyse them for example:

- What is the question?
- How was it asked?
- Who was it asked of?

- Why was it asked of them?
- What is the question trying to achieve?
- How did they answer?
- What was their reaction?
- How did the questioner proceed?
- Do you think they got the answer they wanted?

Can you learn from the style, the content, the delivery? Was the question the right question and was it to the right person at this time? What can you learn from it?

This analysing of questions can be carried out when watching others question in live situations around you, but also on television or radio. There are programmes such as Question Time and Parliamentary Questions in the UK that could be used.

Analyse when questions are asked of you:

- What is your response?
- How do you feel?
- Why have you responded like that?
- Do you feel threatened?
- How do you deal with being threatened?
- What is the person really after achieving?
- Are you helping them achieve what they are after?
- Are you avoiding the question?

It is powerful to play with the subject of questioning. Try different approaches yourself. What works?

Look at the body language of whom you are asking a question?

Try something different. Instead of telling someone to do something see if you can get them to comply with your wishes by asking a series of simple questions. Maybe take a softer approach or a harder approach and see the difference in reactions and answers.

Then try not to ask any questions for a while. How frustrating is it? Are you more or less effective by not asking questions?

Be aware in all situations where a question is being asked. Try to avoid answering on autopilot.

Once you have given the idea of not asking questions a break for a while, force yourself to ask as many questions as possible and see the response, the difference from others. See the gains and benefits to your Personal Knowledge Base (PKB).

Practise, practise and practise. It will make you more effective.
Ask questions to yourself in your mind – practise until you feel comfortable asking questions properly.

Explore firstly in your mind and then openly how you would frame your question and guess the response beforehand. When planning to ask others questions use the five-finger model. Ask yourself the top five likely answers. What would be your response to those five answers?

Rehearse the answers
Were they what you expected?

Make sure whenever you ask questions you have a clear view of the outcome you are trying to achieve. Was the response in line with the outcome you had set yourself before you started?

If not, why not?

Think consciously about questioning
If you can find someone to rehearse with, do it. Ask them to role play. Ask them your questions in different ways. Get some feedback on how they felt.

These are all techniques in becoming better at questioning. Take the theory and practise.

Be confident in yourself. In the business community, I have noticed that many people hold back from asking questions because they might appear silly! Really! This is unlikely to be the case. You do not, cannot and should not, know it all. This mistake is abundant in business. It is not a sign of weakness to need knowledge rather than always have it. In fact, people usually look up to those that seek advice, and people like to be involved. Involve them and ask questions. You do not know it all and you remain at a disadvantage if you pretend you do.

Ask those dumb questions and play devil's advocate. When you do this people will respond to you positively and you will grow in stature.

Understand what is good. When you see examples of good questioning understand why they are good examples. Become a critic of questioning. Log your notes on a learning tree (mind map of learning points).

We are discouraged, even when young, from asking questions because people often don't know the answers. Don't be discouraged if people often do not want to answer them and use an avoiding tactic. They may have their own reasons but it is very unlikely to be anything personal.

Expect some kickback as it is very likely there will be some kickback: "What is it to you?" or "Why do you want to know?" Do not get upset or riled by the kickback; take it in your stride. With difficult subjects, people will not want to answer or may not be able to answer the questions and an easy way to stop a questioner is to become hostile.

I do the opposite to stopping. The more hostile someone becomes the more I continue to ask those awkward questions as it usually means I am getting towards my objective. Obviously take care that it is not the way you are asking the questions that is causing the hostility. If you are hostile with your technique it will often drive hostility back. Remember the whole objective of questioning is to achieve your required outcome. If you are not working towards that outcome then stop asking the questions. Focus on that outcome.

Becoming an effective questioner is not an easy task but it is something that you can learn over time by practice.

The local education authority hates me

I was a governor of a secondary school when I was in my twenties and we were asked to attend a conference where a very senior official from the Local Education Authority was speaking. During the talk, I became annoyed at his insistence that it was against the law to have "Any Other Business" on a governing body agenda. I could not believe there was such a law and felt they were imposing on schools because they wanted control over each governing body. The Local Education Authority used to have to be sent the agenda in advance. Obviously "Any Other Business" topics are not laid out before the meeting and so the LEA could not see them. Hence the comment and their feeling regarding loss of control.

> *This gentleman said it was "against the law" to have Any Other Business on the agenda. It was a clear statement and during questions, with 300 other governors in the room, I simply requested the act and reference stating that AOB was not allowed. I could not believe it was against the law. The gentleman fobbed me off! I asked again and was put down. I asked a third time and still did not get a response. At this point, I decided to leave it alone. I did not believe the gentleman, though. I felt he was lying for his own hidden agenda whether for good or bad.*
>
> *To my surprise another governor popped up and asked the same question, then another. In the end, the senior official had to admit it was not "against the law" but against the local education policy. If you don't mind me saying these are very different things!*
>
> *I am not sure I made a friend that day but it certainly demonstrated once more the power of asking a simple question. What was my motive? I do not believe that any individual should so blatantly mislead people.*

So practise and consciously analyse questions put to you along with the answer given. Use the knowledge in this book as part of that analysis and it will take you on an amazing journey of enlightenment in the questioning and answering dynamic.

I will also introduce to you a specific process I call the Advanced Power Questioning Framework in Section IV. This framework will give you a proven and very tangible process to follow.

In summary, then, to become better at asking questions:

- Learn the Advanced Questioning Framework, Section IV.

- Analyse the way questions are put and answered at every opportunity, and
- Practise, Practise, Practise:
  * practise setting objectives;
  * practise understanding the responses;
  * practise the different styles and approaches;
  * practise framing questions;
  * practise asking questions in different ways;
  * practise until the conscious becomes the subconscious and do not underestimate the power of this experiential learning.

Summary of Section III

This section took the knowledge from style, content and delivery in Section II and focused more on how to answer questions in an effective way, although later in the book I have included some additional frameworks that will also help you become more effective at both questioning and responding to questions.

Whilst Chapter 6 described how to answer questions better, Chapter 7 gave some great methods, tips and techniques on how to avoid answering questions.

Chapter 8 then approached methods on how to improve your own skill at questioning.

Section IV

FRAMEWORKS FOR EFFECTIVE QUESTIONING

This section contains some well-known frameworks and some frameworks I have developed over the years. Learn to use them and you will become incredibly good at questioning and thus achieving your objectives.

I have built these frameworks over many years of asking questions in companies from Small Medium Enterprises, SMEs, massive corporate FTSE 100 companies, voluntary organisations and professional bodies. My HR studies and experience have also helped me in forming and then refining the approaches and frameworks.

CHAPTER 9

CRITICAL ROOT QUESTIONING

Over the years it has become apparent to me that people often exaggerate, and pass on information as fact when it isn't. They often believe the information they pass on, based on the flimsiest facts, and then pass on as absolute.

It may not be done in a Machiavellian way or for a Machiavellian reason but because people genuinely believe what they are saying. To accept this information as fact does us a disservice. Over my time in my party political days, when quite often people had an agenda of their own, I started to develop a way of understanding what was real and what was more imaginary, but believed to be real, by those presenting it. This experience grew in the corporate environment and effectively I developed my own way of validating any information that was being presented to me.

In some cases that validation was just the source, i.e.

- How credible the source was.
- Was the source known to me personally?
- Did the source have a history of accurate information?

Then my validation began to extend to:

- whether there was any bias or reason for any bias that I knew or could find out;
- whether they were on the right or left wing of the party, which may help me to understand whether they had any hidden agenda.

Some years later when I read about Critical Thinking it became clear that some of the techniques I was already using had roots in Critical Thinking. From this and further research I named the technique as Critical Root Questioning. This continues to transform my ability to see information more clearly and to get to what I need to know more effectively, something that in the current age of overload of information is imperative to success.

I would, therefore, strongly challenge you to assess all information coming into you, from whatever source, before letting it become knowledge within your Personal Knowledge Base.

Use Critical Root Questioning as a tool in helping you achieve this.

I said I had discovered similarities in my approach to Critical Thinking and so my starting point is to discuss Critical Thinking first and then Critical Root Questioning will be easier to understand.

What is Critical Thinking?

Critical Thinking was first developed by Socrates around 2,500 years ago in 400 BC as a method of probing people who could not justify their knowledge rationally.

The idea was to challenge general thinking; to challenge the accuracy and to make sure things that were being said or seen had a more completeness about them, rather than just being taken at face value.

Socrates suggested deep questioning was needed. When we offer information we assume someone will automatically accept what we say. Why? Did we accept the world is flat? Well, for a long while we did but then Socrates questioned it and from that questioning came the fact that actually, the world is round. Is it? Are you sure? How do you know? Who says so? Are they credible? Nowadays with travel I suggest we have proof, or do we?

> ### *Driving school*
>
> *I undertook a special driving course at which the instructor was most adamant that a dual carriageway speed limit was only seventy when there was a physical solid barrier and not if it had a grass verge between the carriageways. I even double-checked this information with her and had a specific road in mind. A year or so later when driving down the road I was proven wrong when my friend and colleague, Matt, presented the Highway Code version which made it clear it just had to be a central reservation. I thought I had a credible source, double-checked the meaning and put it incorrectly into my knowledge base.*

Even these days people say the camera never lies and I would agree but it is the interpretation that we put on the picture that can tell us a story or lead us to inaccurate information.

So what is Critical Thinking? To a large degree it is thinking based on:

- rationality, logic and not emotion, including one's own self-deception of knowledge, logic or emotion;

- seeking and checking the evidence, following it through to its conclusion;
- understanding motives and bias;
- being open-minded and being able to evaluate different viewpoints, different worldviews;
- being disciplined, precise, meticulous and comprehensive in analysing what is being presented;
- being sceptical and testing assumptions;
- being aware that the interpretation of those facts will rarely be totally accurate even if the facts are;
- testing the reasoning behind why someone believes what they claim;
- challenging your own beliefs and your own knowledge.

Socrates sought clarity and logic, questioning common beliefs and biased views.

Critical Thinking will allow you to sift through and distinguish the knowledge that is reasonable and logical from that which might be appealing but has no grounding and often is accepted because of being comfortable to our own view.

Evidence will always help but so will background knowledge. Things are usually very different from how they appear and a trained eye will have a completely different view. This is because a person with a trained eye can more accurately understand information being put forward. However, even if you know nothing about a subject, Critical Thinking will help you through by:

- thinking systematically;
- enabling you to trace implications broadly and deeply; and
- making sure you go beyond the surface of what is offered.

Do not just accept what is said. Think things through in a process of Critical Thinking for building your own considerable power. Francis Bacon, an English philosopher, thought that our minds, left to their own devices, developed bad habits which he believed led to false or misleading views. He believed our mind would trick itself into all sorts of things. Will it?

Tricking ourselves is often done by well-meaning assumptions. Even those that are already systematically challenged.

> **Shorts or swimming trunks**
>
> *I was on a skiing holiday recently with my son's school. One of the youngsters, Casper, said that he had overheard that no one was allowed in the local swimming pool unless they had Speedos. I asked where he got his information and he told me he had overheard it. I asked him whether he felt that was "reasonable" and how many people have Speedos these days. He sought to check it and found that any type of "swimming trunk" was acceptable but not shorts. Now that seems more reasonable.*

It is healthy to question and doubt all information until it has gone through the systematic reflection process called Critical Thinking.

So analyse and assess for:

- Clarity
- Accuracy
- Relevance
- Depth
- Breadth
- Logicality

Do not necessarily accept things at face value. If you decide you do not need a definitive answer on a subject then you need explore it no further. However, do not accept it as knowledge but as information that might need verification some day.

Remember all reasoning comes from worldview and all reasoning processes should lead to the achievement of goals and objectives.

So to transfer information to knowledge, to be placed in your Personal Knowledge Base (PKB), then question and interpret:

- the ends and objectives sought to giving out this information;
- the status and wording of questions;
- the sources of information and fact;
- the method and quality of information collection (Was it by force or coercion?);
- the mode of judgement and reasoning used;
- the concepts that make that reasoning possible;
- the assumptions that underlie the concepts in use;
- the implications that follow from their use;
- the point of view or frame of reference within which reasoning takes place;
- the fundamentals of the information;
- whether there is more than one view of this information;
- how you can verify the information;
- what assumptions have been used;
- what is implied in the information;
- whether this is consistent throughout the information, or contradictory;
- how you could check the accuracy of the data;
- what else is implied; and
- whether the source is credible.

So how do you validate information to make it knowledge? The best way is to boil that information down as far as possible to the very roots.

Critical Root Questioning in Detail

Critical Root Questioning is to get as near as you can to certainty and clarity around the information being presented, in the time available to you.

Getting to the very roots requires us to:

- test the information to establish whether it is reasonable;
- check for how logical it is;
- see if there is any bias behind the information;
- test the assumptions that the information is built upon;
- understand the environment surrounding the information being presented;
- check the completeness of the information;
- identify the credibility of the sources;
- check for the relevance of the information in relation to your goal or objective;
- hypothesise with knowledge already understood; and
- find additional evidence which will help to build a more solid foundation and prove or disprove the hypothesis.

To get to the roots you may need to get further information in addition to that being presented to you.

When I am presenting any information to someone I try to carry out this analysis myself including challenging, well-founded assumptions of my own. Then I lay bare those assumptions to the person being presented to in the expectation that this will allow further credibility to the information being presented.

Test the information to establish whether it is reasonable.

Let's explore some of the sorts of question you might ask:

- Does the information sit true with everything else you know? Your own worldview?
- How does it sit with the evidence presented?
- What is the actual rationality behind it?
- How does it compare with your input regarding your senses; touch, smell, sight, sound ?
- Would/does it stand up with other people?
- Do you accept the reasons put on the table? Why?
- Have you or can someone provide you with examples?
- How do you know that this is the case?
- What evidence can you provide to support that it is reasonable/ rational?
- Why do you think it would work like this?
- Why have you come to this conclusion?
- How do you know your judgement is sound?

Test the source for credibility:

- What do they believe? What is their worldview?
- How are their beliefs relevant to this information?
- Why do they believe it?
- How does this relate to what you know about them?
- How does this relate to things that have happened in the past?
- Or things that you know are going to happen in the future?

Test it for logic:

- Does it hold up under questioning?
- Is there consistency in the logic?
- Does it follow in logical steps? Does it flow?
- Have you explored all of the avenues which might have holes?
- How could you challenge the information?
- What evidence can you provide to support that it is logical?
- What caused it? What might cause it?
- Why would this cause it?
- What might it cause?

Look for bias:

- What do you know about the source of the information?
- Are they an expert? Who says? What is their credibility?
- Do they or are they likely to have a hidden agenda?
- Why might they want you to know this particular information?
- Why might they know information or want to know?

For example, throughout my life, as we all have, I have come across all types of careers where experts have presented to me, e.g. Doctors, dentists, nurses, trainers, teachers and it has become clear to me that "expertise" is a continuum. Is a doctor just qualified as qualified as an expert who also trains graduates, responds to papers and presents at conferences or universities?

Test the assumptions that the information is built upon:

- Ask the assumptions the information is built upon.
- What do they already know, or think they know?
- How did they work through the assumptions?

- Ask "If you were a little unsure about anything to do with this what would it be?".
- What evidence do you have that it is not an assumption?
- What would happen if…? Challenge the assumption.
- Why do you agree with the assumption?

Understand the environment surrounding the information being presented:

- Who do they work for?
- What is currently in the PESTLE environment that might be relevant? PESTLE was covered in Section II.

Check the completeness of the information:

- Is all of the information there?
- How do you know if it is all there?
- If there was something missing what would it be?

Assess the credibility of the sources:

- How do you know the source really knows what they are passing on?
- What qualifications do they have?
- Can they prove they have sufficient knowledge in the area?
- How practical is the knowledge or is it just theoretical?
- Did they get it from someone else?
- Is the person prone to exaggeration?
- How long have they been working on it?
- Are they recognised by anyone independent?

Determine how relevant the information is in relation to your goal or objective:

- Do I need to question this deeply? How deeply?
- How does it link in with what I am trying to achieve, my outcome?
- Am I interested in adding this information to my knowledge base or shall I leave it out in the cold?

I would personally add some caution here and say that although everything is worth knowing there is a time constraint on everything. Therefore you only need to test things that are relevant and, at the point when you have established what you need for your goal it is worth moving on to ensure you maximise relevant information within the time available.

Hypothesise with knowledge already understood:

- What do I already know? Does it tie in with the new information?
- Is it completely at odds with my existing knowledge?
- Are there other examples that can be used?
- What is the difference between what you know and the new information?

Find additional evidence which will help to build a more solid foundation and prove the hypothesis:

- How can you prove it?
- What is making it happen like this?
- How do you know this?
- Can you give clear examples?
- What clear evidence can you provide to support it?
- Has it happened before and when and where?

From all of the questions above you start to be able to build some reasoned judgement. Your power and credibility will be increased enormously just by these moves.

In summary, we are questioning:

- the sources of information and fact;
- the method of collection of information;
- the quality of the information collected;
- the basis behind the judgement of the information being presented;
- the reasoning that came to the decision being presented;
- the assumptions that underlie the reasoning;
- the worldview that the reasoning relies upon.

Critical Root Questioning is, therefore, like Critical Thinking, a systematic, disciplined, deep dive into anything you want to explore further.

Critical Root Questioning uses existing principles and your own knowledge, however flawed, to seek out, as near as possible, certainty and clarity.

It relies on the questioner being able to shape questions to more rapidly achieve their aim.

The dual carriageway

In my example of the dual carriageway earlier it could have been essential to understanding the speed on a National Speed Zone, and yet I was left believing incorrect information. This could have meant a heavy fine and three points on my driving licence if I had breached it.

Any person carrying out Critical Root Questioning must be able to, as unemotionally as possible, question reflectively on everything presented to them to their own limits.

When you start to see the success of your using this technique you will wonder how you managed without using it before.

CHAPTER 10

QUESTIONING TO THE VOID

> *"Between stimulus and response, there is a space. In that space lies our freedom and power to choose our response. In our response lies our growth and our happiness."*
>
> Stephen Covey in the *7 Habits of Highly Effective People.* This quote is also credited to psychiatrist Viktor E. Frankl.

Questioning "to the Void" is a type of questioning which is very powerful and I have used in many situations.

The basis is that of simple questioning which builds a story as it goes.

Each link is critical in the story and as the story unfolds it is easy to establish how well known that story is or whether it is a story of make-believe by the person providing it.

It is the technique that is used by journalists and the security services when putting together the pieces of a story.

It is a funnelling or focusing type of questioning and drills down further and further until reaching the point when a desired or required outcome is achieved.

It is a form of convergent questioning.

Take an example:

If you wanted to know whether someone stole something what would you do?

Firstly you could ask them outright. That seems reasonable but it could also mean that you are given a false answer. If you were given a false answer how would you know? You could follow the Critical Questioning Framework or you could try this indirect approach of Questioning to the Void.

Q: So where were you between the hours of 7 and 7.30pm last night (when the theft was alleged to have happened)?

A: At home.

Q: What were you doing at home?

A: I was watching television.

Q: What were you watching?

A: Coronation Street.

Q: Great! Was that the episode where Deirdre married Ken? (A leading question…)

A: Err… (… especially if they were not watching it. Fifty-fifty chance of getting it right but a delay in the answer!)

Q: Where did the wedding take place?

A: Err… (Further delay, sweating, white face unless they know!)

Each question links the question before. They form a web. If the person answering is not being totally truthful or does not really know the subject they are discussing this begins to become clear after about five links.

The length of time between answers begins to rise as the person needs to continue to assess whether their current answer is in line with the answers they have already given.

The person tends to start to sweat and the colour begins to drain from the face if they are misleading or not telling the truth.

A good questioner will be able to follow the questions deep down into the roots and if a person is familiar with their subject or is telling the truth it will roll off the tongue and there will be a minimal delay.

If you are recruiting someone who has done a very similar job it is very easy to use this technique to work through examples.

If you are applying for a project management position it is likely you have done it before.

On your CV it shows a number of projects delivered. So did the person you are interviewing complete those projects? If they project-managed them it would be reasonable for them to know things such as the budget, the staffing levels, the expenditure and issues that they might have come across so that's why we often start there.

So was the project successful? – Just to start the conversation and ease the person in.

- What was the budget?
- How much of that was staff?
- What was the organisation of the project?
- So that means you had twenty staff on the project.
- So your average cost per member of staff was £100K... (does that sound right!!!?)?

And the questioning might go on.

This technique is one I have used many times and has enabled me to be very successful at assessing risk. It does not need to be used for just "catching people out". In fact I have mainly used it for risk assessment and ensuring that projects succeed, and that people succeed in what they are doing and trying to achieve.

CHAPTER 11
THE FIVE WHYS METHOD OF QUESTIONING

This method is incredibly powerful for problem solving as well.

The "Five Whys" is exactly what it says. If you ask a why question five times on the same thread or threads you will be able to get to the very roots of something or indeed a problem.

For instance:

Q: Why was the report not in on time this morning?

A: Because I left it at home.

Q: Why did you leave it at home?

A: Because I was in a rush to leave.

Q: Why were you in a rush to leave?

A: Because I was running late.

Q: Why were you running late?

A: Because I was late out of bed.

Q: Why were you late out of bed?

A: Because the alarm failed to go off.

The root of this, therefore, might be that the report was not in on time because the alarm failed to go off. There may be a further sixth which would be why did the alarm not go off? Probably because you forgot to set it. Either way, the process really works.

Notice each of the answers starts with "because". This is something to be expected.

Take another example where perhaps the knowledge is not fully known.

What may be the answers from someone who did not give their report in on time this morning? The answers may be different. They may be:

- They were late into work.
- They had not done the report.

Why were they late into work?

- The train was cancelled.
- The car would not start.
- They overslept.

Let us just take the first branch: the car would not start.

Why would the car not start?

- The starter motor was jammed.
- There was a short in the electrics.
- The battery gave up.
- There was no petrol in the car.

Why was the starter motor jammed?

- Because it was old.
- It had not had a service recently.
- The starter motor was damaged by using it too often.

Why was there a short in the electrics?

- The car was old.
- It had been through a lot of water.
- It had not been maintained for a while.

Why did the battery give up?

- The car was quite old and the battery had not been replaced.
- There had been minimal maintenance on the battery.
- The water had run out in the battery.
- The connection had become loose.

Notice that as you continue to ask the whys through the roots of the topics there tends to be some recurring themes. In problem solving these can begin to form solutions and give you a good idea of the root cause of the issue or at least the most likely cause.

This process is called the Five Whys and can be a very useful framework. It is, of course, an iterative process where you continue to ask the question "why?" five times down each of the paths.

I use the Five Whys technique tied in with mind mapping or a tree diagram software program which gives a very clear picture of each of the roots being followed.

CHAPTER 12

THE KIPLING TECHNIQUE

The Kipling Technique is another of those divergent and creative techniques.

Rudyard Kipling made up a little poem to remember them but essentially it is asking the questions:

- What?
- Where?
- When?
- How?
- Why?
- Who?

to any situation or problem.

> "I have six honest serving men. They taught me all I knew. I call them what and where and when and how and why and who."

For example:

- What is the problem?
- Where is it happening?
- When is it?
- How can we do something about it?
- Why is the situation occurring?
- Who needs to be involved in the problem?

Take a real example:

Q: What is the problem?

A: I am not able to ski because the snow is melting.

Q: Where is it happening?

A: Three Valleys in the French Alps.

Q: When is it happening?

A: 29th March 2017.

Q: Why is the situation occurring?

A: The sun is very hot and the temperature outside is 23 degrees.

Q: How can we do something about it?

A: Difficult to do much about it but to book a holiday earlier next year.

Q: Who needs to be involved in the problem?

A: The ski tourist company & perhaps the French Tourism Department.

Within those questions, you probably have a very good view of the problem now. Supplementary questions can be asked which would give further detail but these questions provide an excellent clarification of the problem. Lack of clarity of the problem is usually the cause of problems not being solved.

CHAPTER 13
APPRECIATIVE INQUIRY QUESTIONS

Appreciative Inquiring is often used in HR and can be combined with leading questions. The use of Appreciative Inquiry helps facilitate transformational change by bringing out discussion points and leading those discussion points in the direction that you want to take them, but always in a positive way. The use of negative questions here is expressly forbidden.

David Cooperrider and Suresh Srivastva are credited with creating "Appreciative Inquiry" as a method of looking into organisations (1980). They were researching "What's wrong with the human side of the organisation?" at Case Western Reserve University.

They discovered that using a positive approach where people use success rather than dissecting problems can be a very powerful stimulus to change. It stops people from being defensive and creates a desire to join in with change.

It has the additional benefit of building relationships and trust as a group or organisation moves forward.

This in itself helps with an organisation's engagement, something so critical these days.

Thus the process will take someone or a group on a journey together. Often transformational change is brought about because Appreciative Inquiry looks at the good and explores how more, better or good could be.

Appreciative Inquiry works in a very different way to other forms of problem solving. Instead of trying to break down a problem into its constituents it takes a positive angle and builds on that positivity.

This is not an in-depth look at Appreciative Inquiry but to give a taste of where again questioning can really help in a business, creating the future, creating transformational change.

The AI process is often sighted through the 4D process:

- Discovery – This is about identifying and appreciating the things that work and the strengths that exist.
- Dream – This is to imagine what "could or might be" and allows the exploration of the possible.
- Design – This is to design and develop ways of using the best, found through discovery, and the vision of what might be, and creating a different route.
- Destiny – This is to finish the planning and execute the different route.

As with all processes, or change, it's really important to work out the required or expected outcome. What are you trying to achieve with the change?

I continue to call this "Vision" and it will be discussed in greater detail in Chapter 14 "The Advanced Power Questioning Framework".

From the Vision the process is to start talking using open questions, rather than challenging the whole process. It is designed to look at strengths, and not work through, look at or imply any criticism. If someone is taking offence at the questions you are asking it is completely missing the point of Appreciative Inquiry.

The subjects you pick to talk through will depend upon your required outcome.

If you were looking at organisational excellence you might want to start with values, relationships and leadership.

The Discovery work through the AI process then allows you to explore positively all of the strengths of whatever you have chosen as the key subject. Once this Discovery is complete the most positive or the most effective strengths can be chosen, and used, to reach your outcome and to take through to the next stage as part of the Dream process.

This Dream section then discusses what would or could be. Initially, I try to avoid leading the conversation and executing the questioning in a similar way to coaching. However, along with Directive Coaching, discussed in the earlier sections of this book, I do add in leading questions if I feel this will help us get to the outcome. Purist coaches will again criticise this additional intervention.

"So with a stronger team what could we achieve with our monitoring operations? How could we improve things? What more could we do/provide?" Notice the use of open questions trying to solicit discussion. Like coaching, many ideas will emerge and, if possible, it is always worth having a scribe. Someone to record the ideas.

Design, if done in a group, creates a fantastic collaborative approach and a vision that everyone can buy into as they all created it themselves.

Jackie Kelm, *Appreciative Living: The Principles of AI in Personal Life* (Venet Publishers, 2005), sums up Appreciative Inquiry explaining it is:

- a positive, strength-based approach to change;
- finding the best in people and the world around them;
- co-creating inspiring future images;
- focusing on what we want more of; and
- finding and unleashing the positive core.

CHAPTER 14
THE ADVANCED POWER QUESTIONING FRAMEWORK

This chapter will take an in-depth view into a unique way of looking at questioning. I developed this over years of questioning including coaching managers and leaders from small companies all the way through to FTSE 100 companies.

The Advanced Power Questioning Framework is based upon V.A.P.E.R. first introduced in *The Advanced Power State* (Troubador, Feb 2010).

- Vision
- Analysis
- Planning
- Execution
- Review

I have been teaching this V.A.P.E.R acronym, for management and leadership, for more than thirty-five years. It is an absolute fundamental for anyone studying or involved in leadership or management.

Some people who have been managing for years work through this system or approach without even knowing it.

The Advanced Power Questioning Framework Unravelled.

The framework has been put together and used for many years and it works. Initially, it will be a conscious process but very quickly it will become subconscious. It is at this point that it becomes really powerful and you will find your performance improving.

People do not question the concept of V.A.P.E.R: Vision, Analysis, Planning, Execution and Review.

The concept starts with a goal allowing you to analyse where you are and the gap that needs to be filled, as well as creating a clear plan and becoming familiar with the approach you are going to take. Then, of course, carrying out any questioning received. Finally, reviewing the questioning and how it went and then deciding on the next course of action.

Follow the framework using the knowledge and information in the earlier sections of the book for some great results.

Vision
The first stage is Vision. The questions are clear:

- What are you trying to achieve?
- What are your goals?
- What is your purpose?
- Why are you doing it?
- What is your reason for being here?

If you start a journey in a car and do not know where you are going you will not reach the destination. What is your destination? Your desired outcome, of course. There are always reasons why people do things and there is always an outcome or something to be gained. The outcome may be just to have a pleasant drive in the countryside, but it is still an outcome. In this instance a person may not need to know where they are going, but that could be the whole point.

So the same concept of having a vision, a goal, or a purpose applies to questioning. What are the first and most critical things you need to know when looking at forming a question? What are you trying to seek; to solve; to understand by asking the question in the first place?

Take an example:

In the past, I have been criticised for asking questions, where I already know the answers. This has even been fed back to me during a 360-degree feedback process in major corporations.

I do not apologise for it because the answer was not my purpose or goal for asking the question in the first place.

When does a teacher ask a question to which they do not know the answer? Very rarely I suggest.

So why would you ask a question if you did not want an answer?

It may be:

- I am seeking further information around the answer;
- I want to make sure the individual has or knows the answer;
- that you want to influence them;
- you want to develop their vision and values.

This list goes on. What is your purpose for the questioning?

X25 protocol

When I was around twenty-four I went to buy a new computer at a famous computer store. I asked the gentleman selling the computers whether it had an X25 interface. Now you techies out there will know that an X25 interface is nothing to do with computers, but telecommunications. You can imagine my surprise when he came back and said yes! I realised I could not trust anything he said. That was my objective: to see if he was a credible source of information, and by asking something I knew then I would not be fooled by believing something incorrect that I did not know.

Missing £50,000

I was a senior manager in an organisation and one of my team, who was managing a project, came to me and said that a particular stakeholder had spent £50,000 of money, which really belonged in someone else's budget, without that person's authority. Later in the day, both people were at a meeting together. During the meeting, I had the opportunity of asking the project manager, "Who authorised the money to be spent?" The project manager looked at me with complete surprise and a lack of understanding. He knew I knew the answer but as I explained to him later my objective was not to get the answer but to get the person who had spent the money to own up so that the owner of the budget could retrospectively approve it.

In the end it all worked out but I did not need what, on the surface, would have been seen as "the answer".

It is only by working out what you are trying to achieve in the first place that you can start to put together the question(s) in a way that will get you closer to the result you are after.

- Are you inviting someone to something?
- Are you trying to get information about something?
- Are you trying to motivate someone to do something?
- Are you trying to influence someone or get them to think in a certain way?

Knowing what you are trying to achieve is fundamental in all management and leadership, and it applies to getting to the truth and understanding more through questions.

It is also worth noting that what you are trying to achieve is not necessarily the same as what you are trying to find out. So keep your wits about you.

You need to understand both. Where do you want to be at the end of the questioning? Only knowing this will you know when you have arrived.

> **The missing shipment**
>
> *Similar to a story earlier but on a different occasion I once asked someone if a shipment was arriving that day. This was not because I needed to know the answer but because I wanted to bring it to their attention to ensure it had the focus as I needed to get it in urgently. The person went off and chased the order. It was obviously not going to arrive on that day!*

Think about the whole picture and decide what you are after. What is your required outcome, your vision?

Understand your purpose, your vision, first.

Analysis

Once you understand the purpose of asking the question, the next stage is to know where you are.

By knowing where you are currently and already knowing where you want/need to be then you can establish any gap.

To fill in the gap you need to establish:

- where to go to ask the question(s);
- who might know the answer to the question(s);
- who you are going to ask;
- will they enable the objective to be reached?

When you have found who to ask then you need to work out the approach to the questioning.

Perhaps some background knowledge is needed first. In which case where are you going to get that?

Questions such as:

- Are they the right person?
- Why are they the best person to ask?
- What might be their reaction to being questioned on this?
- What follow up question might they/you have?
- What sort of person are they?
- What sort of temperament do they have?
- What is their worldview?
- What is likely to be the best approach to this person or group?

- What is the PESTLE environment in which you are asking the questions?
- Do they/will they know the answers?
- Have you any additional information to help you validate what will be said?
- How will you be sure they know the facts?

This is definitely a candidate for Critical Root Questioning techniques.

What do you think they might know or be able to tell you?

Part of the analysis is to understand who you are questioning. In communications terms that is "Understanding your Audience". What do they know on the subject? How do they think? Take some time to analyse those involved in all of the questions.

Planning

You have established your purpose, your goal, and analysed where you are along with the gap you need to fill. Now comes the time when you need to plan on how you are going to fill the gap or gaps. What style of questioning and the best approach to take are all relevant here.

You should already have an understanding of your audience from the analysis but if you do not, find out about the audience. This will be able to be used in aligning questions later in the framework.

The plan needs to work through:

- the style of the questioning;
- the content or at least type of content; and
- how it is going to be delivered.

These are all covered in Section II.

Have you mapped out the environment; how the person feels; what might be going on around them; their drivers? All of this will be significant when planning the style, content and delivery.

What would be the best approach/style of question?

- Aggressive
- Passive
- Enquiring
- Neutral mediation

Types of questions:
Decide the type/style of question you are going to ask.

Decide the content of your question.

Match the question to the person. Will you get the most from taking a direct approach? Or should you take another approach?

Is it one person? Or a group? Do you have any other information that may allow you to better understand their worldview, their beliefs, how they might respond to different approaches to questioning? All of this information will help in planning the approach for the questioning.

What do you think they are expecting from the discussion or interview that is to take place?

Might they have concerns and might these concerns hold them back from answering?

What is the content likely to be? Is it better to use more complicated words or simpler words?

These days it is more important, than ever, to consider the medium to use.

Consider:

- how do you deliver the question(s); and
- why does the approach change?

How can you change the approach to get the most from asking the questions in either of the follow ways:

- verbal; or
- written?

Both are covered in Section II of this book.

How is your body language going to be on delivery?

- Open?
- Closed?
- Aggressive?
- Passive?
- Submissive?

Are you going to make clear eye contact? Is it with one person or several? Who? Where?

Eye contact, where possible, is key in any communication, and questioning is no exception. Keep eye contact. Evading someone's eyes can be very confrontational. Is that the approach you are planning to take? Is your delivery going to be:

- Enthusiastic?
- Warm?
- Disinterested?
- With a confident tone?
- With an angry tone?

How are you to convey your questions in tone? High pitched or lower pitch? Which method is likely to be more successful?

Change your tone and notice how people change in their response.

All of these things can impact the answer you receive.

And:

- What questions are you going to ask?
- How are you going to ask them?
- Where are you going to ask them?
- How might this play out? Remember the five-finger model.

Would it be useful to have more than one person when asking the questions for follow-ups? Will a group of people have more of the answers you need?

Different types of question can be used and applied to different situations. However, it is not just the different questions that can affect the answers. It can often boil down to the planning of the order in which the different questions are asked.

If there is more than one person involved have you placed yourself so that you can see their eyes interchanging looks when you get to the execution(delivery) stage?

Practice makes perfect! Long has this been known and so rehearse the questions in your mind or better still with someone else.

Execution

Execution is not only about delivering your questions but how it is done. It is about the interaction between individuals.

You will need to tailor your approach to get the most from the responder, and the most towards your goal. Whilst you can plan scenarios, things may not play out entirely as you anticipate or expect them to.

You may need to think on your feet.

This is where the rule of three comes in.

- There is the planned questioner session;
- the delivered session; and
- the recorded session.

In the execution of any plan, it is important to stay flexible and adaptable as you receive more and more answers to your questioning. Your goal will help you stay focused on the end game but executing the plan or re-planning should be an ongoing exercise in your mind.

I often liken questioning to a jigsaw puzzle where each question should give you another piece towards your final outcome. It can also be represented as a tree and often recorded as such, as questioning can build a multiplicity of possibilities. However, all of this should still be working towards your final outcome, putting together the picture of your goal.

When questioning, be observant. Note their response, verbal or other. Pay attention to what they have deliberately not said or avoided. If they have avoided the question ask it another way. If it is avoided again that should give you further information in itself.

Try to establish and understand why they have avoided the question.

Have they actually answered the question so many times they don't want to answer it again or is there another reason? The more trained an individual becomes the more subtly they will be able to avoid answering a question.

Why do they not want to answer? Read between the lines and then test your belief as to why. What are they really saying/communicating? If you are unsure, clarify it with them. Make sure you are clear. Look at Section III for ideas on how people may avoid questions.

The response may be confident or tentative, strong or weak. The tone may be in a specific way telling a specific story. Learn to understand this communication. The words may be long or short. All of these tell a story. Are they looking at you in the eye when they give you the answers? Remember, the eyes are a great source of communication.

Remember, the building of the picture towards your answer is more than just the answer to the words. It is:

- what is said;
- how it is said;
- what is omitted;
- non-verbal communication as well. For example, a person's response may include fidgeting.

You can also use your own PKB, Personal Knowledge Base, to build further on your picture.

Reading the answers

There is no point in asking excellent questions if you struggle to read the answers. All responses tell a story.

- The way the person responds
- The words they carefully use
- What is not said as much as what is said
- The way they move their body

When considering answers also consider those who have had media training. The answers may be very different and the individual will choose their words very carefully. What they are actually saying may be up to you to determine.

- Have they deviated away from the discussion, away from the answer you wanted?
- Did they answer a completely different question?
- Did they answer the question in a vague manner?
- Did they move their body in an awkward way?
- Did they shift from side to side?
- Did they fidget in their seat?
- Did their eyes look at you and then look away?

When you carry out questioning here is a very big tip. Look the person in the eye. This also applies when answering. This will tell the person answering a considerable amount about your resolve to get an answer as hidden subliminal messages will be received by the responder. A "trust" consideration will also be made on the eye contact. Usually, but not always, you will find that the eye contact with a friendly, sincere smile will take away the fear that an individual will naturally have for someone they do not know.

On their own, these things might not mean much but start to put a pattern together and you will find you can read people and then verify your thinking about the non-verbal communication.

Is it a fast, firm, confident response or does it demonstrate hesitation?

What is fiction? Where people actually make things up Critical Root Questioning can help.

I was once told that some people look to the creative side of the brain when they are lying and the factual side when they are recalling from memory. Is there a pattern? A look to the right for creative and left for logical?

What do people think is true and what is not true?

What is built on assumptions?

What confidence/credibility does the person have for you?

Critical Root Questioning will help you understand these questions.

Did someone else tell them something that they now believe to be true?

You already have your PKB, Personal Knowledge Base, to interpret responses, both verbal and non-verbal, to any questions. By building on your existing knowledge you can complete the whole jigsaw, including the use of that background knowledge or perhaps additional research.

Take your own knowledge and add the incoming knowledge and experience and then extrapolate and test the extrapolated theory.

Interpret what people do not say, and test your understanding by playing a scenario back to them.

Use this intelligence and extrapolate to judgements that can be tested.

In the meantime, are you ready for a follow-up question?

Is it a clarification or are you using a summary question?

All of these techniques are described in Chapter 5.

Are you ready for a clarification or follow-up question?

One of your key indicators when receiving a non-verbal answer is a change in behaviour.

Review

A review can be done whilst questioning is still going on and should be iterative. However, at the end, ensure that you have reached your goal. Are you at the end point you set yourself at the beginning of the questioning?

Continue to check the responses and answers you are getting.

- Whilst the execution is going on, review should also be a part of it.
- These answers will help you in the continuing relationship with the responder.
- There is also something about knowing when to stop.

Don't talk out your sale

As managing director I decided to spend a day out with one of my sales agents who was about to make a huge sale for our company. Initially I was extremely impressed. However, once the customer had agreed to buy, the agent kept asking questions even as he was doing the paperwork. Eventually, he asked a question which presented a little doubt to the customer who then said, "Well, let me just think about it." The sale was lost so know when to be quiet.

Have you achieved your objectives? Did you get the answers you needed? Have you managed to influence the person or persons? Is the person going to take action if that was the desired outcome?

Was the style, content and delivery suitable and the best way of achieving those objectives?

Have you verified the information with your own knowledge and entered it into your Personal Knowledge Base (PKB) or is there more to find out?

Note any follow-up you may need to do.

Do you need to talk to someone else?

Do some research and then come back to ask more questions.

Is there another way?

Does the person need time to reflect before a follow-up?

If you have not achieved your objectives was questioning the best way of achieving them? Could or should things have been done a different way?

Can you learn from the experience? How could you do it better next time?

Never underestimate this Review stage of the Advanced Power Questioning Framework.

CHAPTER 15
ADVANCED POWER QUESTIONING FRAMEWORK IN PROBLEM SOLVING

The Advanced Power Questioning Framework linked in with Problem Solving is still wrapped around a simple standard management concept V.A.P.E.R:

- Vision
- Analysis
- Planning
- Execution
- Review

V.A.P.E.R in Problem Solving.

Vision (goal setting)

- Write down the problem you are really trying to solve and the goal. What are you aiming for?
- What will things really look like once the problem is solved?

It is essential to articulate the actual problem in writing.

Then ask relevant questions. The processes such as Critical Root Questioning, Five Whys, Kipling Technique, and Appreciative Inquiry can all be used to focus on Problem Solving.

Once you have your goal, carry out the analysis of where you are and the gap you need to fill.

Analysis:

- Where are we now?
- What is the gap between the vision and where we are now?
- What are the possible causes for this gap?
- What are the most likely root causes (which can be done by root cause analysis)?
- What can we do about the root causes? (This is a creative piece.)

The creative divergent phase can be done with divergent questioning. Ask about the possibilities. What could we do?

Planning:

- What can I do to change the situation, to eliminate or reduce the impact of the root causes?
- What actions do I need to carry out?
- In what order do these actions need to be carried out?
- Who needs to carry them out and by when do they need to be done?

Execution:
This is a step people often lose track of… Take action!

Review:

- Monitor continuously.
- Where am I in terms of my goal?
- Have I achieved or reached the goal or do I need to go through the process again?

The last few paragraphs are not designed to make you an excellent problem solver but are designed as an example of how different questioning approaches can be used at different times to achieve different results.

Detailed problem solving is a book in itself and so the ideas above are designed to give you a flavour.

CHAPTER 16

RECRUITING EFFECTIVELY USING THE APQ FRAMEWORK

Examples of really effective questions and approaches for job interviewing

In any organisation, recruitment should be the number one priority. In most companies and organisations, it is the cost of people which remains the highest expense and the highest risk to the success of the business.

In all my years in HR and dealing with people and organisations there has been a radical change and part of that is understanding engagement. Engagement does not start at the point someone starts with the company. It starts when they first have a connection with the company or have seen a job advertised.

How you deal with recruitment has an effect on that person for the rest of their employment and sometimes their lives. So make that experience a great experience.

I recruit on the basis of the five A's:

- Attitude
- Aptitude
- Ability
- Agility
- Adaptability

If the attitude is not one that blends in with your company then the relationship with the company and the other people who work in it is doomed before that individual even starts work.

If you are recruiting for a job which requires experience then test the experience.

My Advanced Power Recruiting Process works on the basis of defining a key number of questions.

There are seven stages in getting to write some thorough questions for recruitment and this is about being prepared:

Stage 1 – An introductory job description

The introductory job description needs to really sell the job. Whatever the job is it must appeal to someone. So make it appeal to them.

For many years I have seen paragraphs in job advertisements such as:

"Person wanted to work in the Compliance Department to carry out admin tasks." Clearly, that does not sound very interesting. To me this role is about filing, shuffling papers and doing very boring things… Well, that is what someone will probably take away.

"A thorough individual is needed to work in our vital Compliance Department ensuring we are able to continue to deliver to our clients." Now that sounds a bit more interesting, doesn't it?

Stage 2 – A detailed job description

Then there is a need for a detailed job description. Now many would say you can go overboard with this and whilst you may not want to give it all to a possible candidate if you can produce a strong detailed job description of the ideal person it can be used in the interviewing to measure against.

Stage 3 – The advert

Once you have completed the job description you may want to put an advert together or this may have formed part of the introductory description. Make it dynamic and exciting. Get someone from the marketing team to write it.

Stage 4 – The PDP (Personal Development Plan)

This will consist of the first year's objectives. What do you want the jobholders to achieve? How are you going to measure them? The PDP may include specific targets or may also have an element about behaviours.

I am not suggesting that this is discussed in great detail at the interview but you do need to have an idea of what will be required of them, and it will aid them hitting the ground running much faster.

The job description will help.

Stage 5 – Write the questions

So take all of the above documents and write questions which allow you to understand whether or not the person fulfils the criteria.

Where is it you wish them to have experience?

Use the technique of Questioning to the Void to find out how involved they have been in things.

Use the other techniques described in Section IV.

Use the:

- Introduction job description
- Full job description
- Advert
- Personal objectives for the year ahead

Then form questions using the style, content and delivery techniques described in Section II.

Stage 6 – The environment

Provide a good environment to ask the questions. Often I use assessment days where someone gets to really know the department, the people, the company and has an opportunity to carry out examples of the type of work they will be doing. However, this is not always possible and sometimes the old-fashioned interview approach needs to be used.

Provide a comfortable and quiet room, not a coffee shop.

It is important to note that the people who get jobs in interviews are often those that can interview well and sales people.

Sales is all about matching the needs of the customer with the products or services you supply. Be aware that you are getting what you really want or need.

Questioning should help establish this.

Stage 7 – Review

Review the questions and the responses. Did you achieve what you wanted?

See the comments on the review section of the Advanced Power Questioning Framework.

Apply those ideas here.

> **Governor recruitment again, please!**
>
> *I was a governor for eleven years and during that period I sat on an interview panel for a new head of the school. We went through all of the candidates primarily trying to ensure that we picked one who would take the school forward, in the culture we wanted the school to continue to adopt, and to modernise it. We had a clear mind to what we wanted but all of the applications put forward by the Local Education Authority, LEA, were interviewed and not suitable. The governors were told, "Well, that's what there is and you have to choose." I rejected this out of hand. They were all good candidates but not right for this school. I objected and said we would run the process again. The LEA informed me this was not possible but I refused to agree and managed to convince enough governors to support my view. We refused to take on any of the heads, ran the process again for the term after, and employed a fantastic head, Peter, who was absolutely right for the school and stayed with the school for over eight years.*

Close

Get the right person. They are always out there in the job pool. Do not get someone just because it is convenient.

The questions will help you to understand if the person is suitable.

Summary of Section IV

In Section IV some unique frameworks have been presented. I have tried not to repeat the ideas in the different frameworks and models but to call on the skills you have picked up from the rest of the book. The frameworks are just that; a framework. Fill in the framework with your specific situation and you will find your abilities in questioning improve and thus your success will grow.

There are other situations where applying questioning in the manner of the Advanced Power Questioning Framework will reap great results. Situations such as workshops, facilitating, as well as coaching as already described, are some examples.

Use your imagination to create further ideas and uses.

SUMMARY

When I first set out to write this book it seemed like a small undertaking but the more I researched and provided the copy for the way I handle questioning the more I realised it was an almost never-ending subject.

I sought to write it in a way that utilised anecdotes to prove the content and I do hope you enjoyed them. However, even if you did not enjoy the anecdotes there are some great ideas for you to take away.

Section I provided an introduction and explained just how important questioning is in a day-to-day environment and how it can really add to your success. Section II started to build on the elements of questioning and answering that are often missed. It also included the Immersed Questioning Environment and the relationship between the different parties involved. It worked through the constituents of questions including the breakdown of style, content and delivery.

Section III then worked through answering questions effectively and avoiding answering questions effectively! Both are valid. It then went on to look at how to improve your capability at asking questions. Techniques and ideas to help you in this area were also included.

Section IV introduced some unique frameworks, models and tools to become better at questioning. There is no doubt that these techniques work. Some were created by me personally and some by other individuals as discussed in each chapter.

Remember, it is recognised that people tend to look up to and respect questioners more and the results from good questioners are better than poor questioners.

Questioning, in the right manner, can lead to a greater level of trust of you, especially if a level of humbleness is contained within the approach to questioning. This can improve business performance but also you yourself and the value you continue to provide.

So to finish off, firstly I hope the book has entertained you but I also hope it has inspired you to take questioning more seriously, to analyse where you are and to learn new approaches to improve your overall value in whatever you do.

Finally, I would like to leave you with the suggestion, "Have fun doing it".